At
Your
Own
Risk

Other Books by Derek Jarman
Published by the University of Minnesota Press

Chroma
Dancing Ledge
Kicking the Pricks
Modern Nature
Smiling in Slow Motion

At Your Own Risk

A Saint's Testament

Derek Jarman

University of Minnesota Press

Minneapolis

Originally published in 1993 by The Overlook Press, Woodstock, New York

First University of Minnesota Press edition, 2010

Published by the University of Minnesota Press
111 Third Avenue South, Suite 290
Minneapolis, MN 55401-2520
http://www.upress.umn.edu

Library of Congress Cataloging-in-Publication Data

Jarman, Derek.
At your own risk : a saint's testament / Derek Jarman.
p. cm.
Originally published: Woodstock, N.Y. : Overlook Press, 1993.
ISBN 978-0-8166-6592-1 (pb : alk. paper)
1. Jarman, Derek, 1942–1994. 2. Motion picture producers
and directors—Great Britain—Biography. 3. Gay men—Great Britain—Biography.
4. AIDS (Disease)—Patients—Great Britain—Biography. I. Title.
PN1998.3.J3A3 2010
791.4302'33092—dc22
[B]
2010000615

Printed in the United States of America on acid-free paper

The University of Minnesota is an equal-opportunity educator and employer.

16 15 14 13 12 11 10   10 9 8 7 6 5 4 3 2 1

Contents

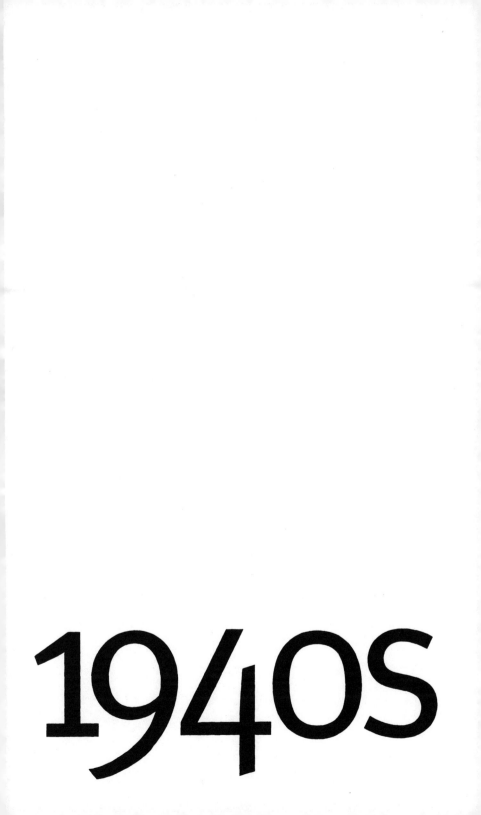

1940S

A FIRE IN THE NIGHT

The cold night breeze is up. It's two hours since you went to bed. I pick my way through the wood in the shimmering orange light, over the dead autumn leaves in their ghostly marbled pattern.

The blue smoke from the bonfire drifts in the branches, silhouetted against the clear winter night. A jet roars through the cold stars. I hug myself to keep warm.

At the fire's edge strangers stand motionless. The trunk of a great tree burns, an open book where the saw has cut five fiery wounds. Ember pages shoot showers of sparks high into the night. My mind flows with the blue flames that flicker across the wood. Fire hisses the winter death of the great tree, the circles of its years reduced to ash. We are all dying here with the old tree, shedding its years to warm us.

A man strikes a light for himself in the night when his sight is quenched. Living, he touches the dead in his sleep. Waking, he touches the sleeper.

- Heraclitus

Landscapes of time, place, memory, imagined landscapes. *At Your Own Risk* recalls the landscapes you were warned off: Private Property, Trespassers will be Prosecuted; the fence you jumped, the wall you scaled, fear and elation, the guard dogs and police in the shrubbery, the byways, bylaws, do's and don'ts, Keep Out, Danger, get lost, shadowland, pretty boys, pretty police who shoved their cocks in your face and arrested you in fear.

Last night was the first night of winter. We flew a kite round the moon, loop-the-loop, the leaves were falling off the trees.

I don't know how long I spent there. My mind was racing. I was writing my book in the dark, angrily.

ANY OLD MARRIAGE

Squadron-Leader L. E. Jarman, R.A.F., and Miss E. E. Puttock.
The marriage arranged between Squadron-Leader Lancelot Elworthy

3

Jarman, R.A.F., second son of Mr. and Mrs. H. E. Jarman, of Christchurch, New Zealand, and Elizabeth Evelyn (Betty), daughter of the late Harry Litten Puttock, of Calcutta, and Mrs. Puttock, of Northwood, will take place quietly at Holy Trinity Church, Northwood, on March 31, at 2 p.m. All friends are welcome at the church.

I was born on the 31 January 1942 at seven thirty in the morning at the Royal Victoria Nursing Home in Northwood.

For the first twenty-five years of my life I lived as a criminal, and the next twenty-five were spent as a second-class citizen, deprived of equality and human rights. No right to adopt children - and if I had children, I could be declared an unfit parent; illegal in the military; an age of consent of twenty-one; no right of inheritance; no right of access to a loved one; no right to public affection; no right to an unbiased education; no legal sanction of my relationships and no right to marry. These restrictions subtly deprived me of my freedom. It seemed unthinkable it could be any other way, so we all accepted this.

In ancient Rome, I could have married a boy; but in the way that ideals seem to become their shadows, love came only to be accepted within marriage. Since we could not be married, we could not fall in love. Since we could not fall in love, we were not loved.

SODOM, SOD'EM

The sin of the people of Sodom was a lack of hospitality - they rejected God's angels and for this they were punished. The myth of sexual licence is a myth. The lack of hospitality that we have received in my lifetime reveals a true Sodom in the institutions of my country.

Heterosoc, imprisoned by monogamy in the ruins of romantic love, is quite dumbfounded when faced with our plurality. We are the 11,000 angels dancing on the head of a pin.

THE INTRODUCTION

My book is a series of introductions to matters and agendas unfinished. Like memory, it has gaps, amnesia, fragments of past, fractured present.

To those who have not lived it, it might appear opaque; those of us who are living it will recognise the map.

My doctor says people have said to him that PWAs whom he has also treated for venereal disease, should be locked up - as they do in Havana.

The epidemic has spawned more hatred - we were locked in prison before it started, now we are to be placed in isolation. Am I to believe I am the delinquent you say I am? Or do I throw it back in your face?

How can I be open and honest if defenders of an outdated morality are not prepared to undertake a rudimentary re-evaluation of their prejudice, because to do so forces them to talk of matters they are unwilling to address?

Yet, how can I talk about responsibility when there is no information on these matters, and none of our political parties will give a lead?

How can the young express their sexuality openly and safely when the age of consent is 21?

This book, you can be certain, will not be in the school library. Youth will be told it isn't 'normal'. Their elders, the pillars of society, will sooner see them die than be happy.

The problem of so much of the writing about this epidemic is the absence of the author. How would the much-criticised article 'Gay Abandon' in the *Guardian* have read if it were in the first person?

'*I* am maladjusted', '*I* am the end of the line.'

It is no good alerting the 'public' whilst distancing yourself.

I have frequently been stopped by anguished young men, some still in school, who have confided they are HIV+. I am usually the first person they have told. There is so little support in the home.

They and I have had to struggle with a lack of understanding; have had to piece together a life under a great dark cloud of censure and ignorance. They and I are frightened of you, ourselves and the virus.

Five years ago in 1986, I walked into a crowded room aware that everyone knew my HIV status. Should I kiss old friends on the cheek? They might not yet know they could come to no harm.

Years passed, I strove for the celibacy of a saint. Around me people were enjoying themselves. They didn't seem prepared to take the epidemic on board, left that to us. We were given so much practical advice, but so little understanding. Understanding does not appear on the drugs list, but is as vital as a hospital drip.

Understand that sexuality is as wide as the sea.

Understand that your morality is not law.

Understand that we are you.

Understand that if we decide to have sex whether safe, safer, or unsafe, it is our decision and you have no rights in our lovemaking.

Sexual encounters were nice in the Palace, nasty in the park.

I was once given a blow-job by a male nurse while attending a clap clinic, he said: 'I'll just have to give myself a jab, but it's worth it'.

I am the man who kissed in that *Guardian* photograph which was captioned '*Kiss of death?*' If that was the way *that* paper saw me, what hope had I in the tabloids?

I kissed him. He said: 'Suck my cock - you have the dick of death'.
'Let me fuck you'
'O.K.'
Death Fuck - What a great splash for the tabloids.

6

22ND DECEMBER 1986

NOTHING TO BE AFRAID OF? ARE THESE WORDS TOO BRAVE?

The young doctor who told me this morning I was a carrier of the AIDS virus was visibly distressed. I smiled and told her not to worry, I had never liked Christmas. I had put on my dark black overcoat to walk to the hospital. Wearing it at my father's funeral a few weeks ago I looked more sombre than the undertakers. It gave me confidence for this meeting.

As I walked up the freezing street against the tide of Christmas shoppers I thought it was inconceivable I could have avoided the virus, though I had avoided the test for as long as was decently possible. Earlier this year the doctor had suggested I took it; at the time I was coping with the furore that the showing of *Jubilee* on Channel 4 had stirred up: 4am death threats on the phone. I felt insecure. I saw the news leaked to the *Sun* and the *Star* with visions of ending up as part of the daily diet of terror that sells these malevolent and jaundiced newspapers.

It was almost with relief that I listened to the doctor's catalogue of do's and don'ts - shaving, hairdressing, all the little details (soap and water it seemed eliminated the virus outside the body) - but for all of medicine you might as well just wash your mouth out with carbolic.

Walking back down Tottenham Court Road from the hospital, I thought how fortunate to be forewarned so that one can wind one's life up in an orderly fashion. The finality of it seemed attractive.

As I joined the crowds at Oxford Street, I thought - could my perception of all this change, could I fall in love with it again as I did when I left home early in the sixties? The sun came out briefly, the thin wintry sun, so low in the sky it blinds you. The wind seemed colder than ever. I stopped at the stationer's and bought a daybook for 1987 and a scarlet form to write out a will.

LITTLE HEATH 1991

We wandered from the path and got lost in the woods. He stopped, turned and put his arms round me. He had a day's growth, avoided a kiss, undid his jeans and slipped out of them.

'Put on a condom and fuck me.'

'OK' I said knowing that I would never make it; I couldn't get a hard-on for the life of me in this cold. I held him against a tree: young, stocky and firmly built. If only things were different. Overwhelmed with frustration I said:

'I'm sorry I can't fuck you, but I couldn't think of anything sweeter.'

'Why?'

'I'm HIV+, and it's too much of a risk, I can't get a hard-on, let alone put a condom on in this cold.' The cold was a good excuse.

'What's your name?'

'Duncan.'

'How old are you?'

'Twenty-three... You're the first person who has told me he was HIV+.'

'Well, you should know the risk. How often do you come here?'

'Often. I love being fucked... You're really funny.'

We stayed there, holding each other for several minutes; then I said,

'I haven't a clue where I am. Could you show me the way back?' He did.

'All the best,' I said as we parted.

'Thanks'.

The painter Duncan Grant told my friend Simon that he cruised the Heath at the turn of the century.

The Heath no more belongs to the people of Hampstead than the Palace of Westminster belongs to the people of Westminster.

OUR SERVANTS CANNOT LOOK SEX IN THE FACE, THE HOUSE OF COMMONS IS A QUEER OLD PLACE.

The death penalty for buggery was abandoned after 1836, abolished in 1861 in England, and in 1889 in Scotland, to be replaced by penal servitude of between ten years and life.

In 1885, the La Bouchere amendment criminalised all homosexual acts in public or private which resulted in a series of trials - the most famous of which is that of Oscar Wilde. It wasn't until 1967 that this legislation was repealed.

Queerbashing is institutionalised in every walk of British life; if it wasn't the newspapers couldn't make capital out of it.

In a nation of the sexually paralysed...

There are no Queer judges.

No Queer churchmen.

No Queers in the City.

No Queers in the Forces.

No Queers in the Lords.

One MP.

One sportsman.

Three pop stars.

Six theatre queens.

Eighteen signatories to a letter in the *Guardian*.

Myself.

...and a few friends.

Why should I drag myself into all this? If I remained silent like the rest of them I could remain the likeable one.

Overheard in a bar:
'What happened to Derek Jarman?'
'The virus attacked his brain and he saw clearly, dear.'

MY GHOSTLY EYE

Shall I begin on the day that I was overwhelmed by guilt? I had survived. So many of my friends caved in under the hate; I have known men to die for love but more to die for hate. As the years passed, I saw in the questioner's eyes the frustrations of coming to terms with life; are you still here? Some were brutally frank: 'When are you going to die?'

Didn't you know I died years ago with David and Terry, Howard, the two Pauls. This is my ghostly presence, my ghostly eye. 'I had AIDS last year,' I said with a smile and they looked at me as if I was treating their tragedy flippantly. 'Oh yes, I had AIDS last year. Have you had it?'

Now it doesn't matter when I die, for I have survived.

'What are you doing next, Mr. Jarman?' What comes after, after, after, that's the problem when you survive.

Now I understand my father very well. I can feel for him. He flew those bombing missions at the war's height and after that his focus blurred in the slough of the everyday. Why did you fight for this grey street, Dad? This small office? This fax? This computer?

It's been five years now and I still return to the ABC of HIV. Talk of condoms, safe, safer, safest sex again and again. The papers act delinquent, put the clock back to sell a fear, if you open up to them sure enough they'll shoot you down. Well, we knew that would happen.

ARREST THAT MAN... TOM DRIBERG MP, 1943

I was walking along Princes Street towards my hotel. The war was still on, and the whole city was blacked out. In such dim lighting as there was, one could just make out the forms of passers-by - and I bumped into a tall figure in a foreign naval uniform. One of us struck a match to light cigarettes.

He was a Norwegian sailor, typically Scandinavian in appearance, flax-en-haired and smilingly attractive. He may have had a few drinks too: he was eager for anything, and perhaps lonely (loneliness is as strong an incentive, often, as lust).

I recalled that there was an air-raid shelter under the gardens a few yards from where we were standing. Neither of us could speak the other's language, but he readily came down to the shelter with me.

Down there it was completely dark, but another match showed a bench running along one side of the shelter...

In a matter of seconds he had slipped his trousers half-way down, and was sitting on the bench, leaning well back. We embraced and kissed, warmly enough, but my interest was concentrated lower down, on a long, uncircumcised, and tapering, but rock-hard erection; and I was soon on my knees. Too concentrated, and too soon perhaps; for in a few moments the stillness of the shelter was broken by a terrifying sound - the crunching, very near at hand, of boots on the gravelled floor. Instantly the blinding light of a torch shone full on us, and a deep Scottish voice was baying, in a tone of angry disgust: 'Och, ye bastards - ye dirty pair o' whoors...' No concealment was possible... and I stood up, to confront a young Scottish policeman... with an older Special Constable lurking behind him.

- RULING PASSIONS, TOM DRIBERG

OLD MYTHS AND TALL STORIES

There was always a mythic past, for my generation it was the war. My elders told me of their sexual experiences in the war, how liberating it had been. It was a world that depended on economic disadvantage; the sol-diers and the sailors were prepared to spend a night with them for ten bob, until the government upped the pay of the forces and ended National Service.

The wild stories I heard when I came to London were about guardsmen and sailors - violations of Heterosoc. There were guardsmen's pubs. You had to be middle-aged and rich in that world.

In Rome, years later, I met a man who had an order with the local barracks. The Duty Sergeant used to send him four or five young conscripts, he'd take their clothes off and put them into immaculate white dressing gowns and cook for them. 'Which one do you like Derek?' I was tongue-tied.

Italy was like that. I was 'raffled' by a group of young conscripts in Ischia; and won by a delightful boy from Sicily who, as he came all over me, remarked that he was returning home to get married in a few days.

There were scandals involving the Guards, even as recently as the eighties. The boys who guarded the Bank of England were known as 'the bum boys'. The Guards were run as rent boys for the privileged, members of parliament and the aristocracy. The Queers who you never met.

These people weren't 'out'. They were never seen in the bars. As a young MP, Harold Macmillan - who was expelled from Eton for an 'indiscretion' - used to spend nights at the Jermyn Street Baths; anyone who went to them would have been propositioned during the course of an evening. I went there myself on two or three occasions. They were a well-known hangout: dormitory beds and steam rooms full of guardsmen cruising.

There was a link between the military and rent. Waterloo Station was very cruisy in the fifties. The sailors who were Queer or wanted to make a few bob used to miss the last trains back to Portsmouth and catch the milk train after sex with a punter early in the morning. Class was central to these liaisons.

Churchill remarked the traditions of the Navy were rum, mutiny and sodomy.

The military have always been Queer, at least the best of them: Alexander the Great, Julius Caesar, Richard the Lionheart, Fredrick the Great, Gordon, Kitchener, Mountbatten, and Alexander of Tunis

REAL GREEK MUSIC

When I was 23, I spent a summer in Greece. One night in Rhodes, rather lost, I sat on the quay watching local lads catch octopus.

Several ships of the Greek Navy were in port. A young Lieutenant in immaculate white accompanied by a regular sailor stopped and asked me where I was from.

When I told him I was from England, he said: 'Would you like to hear the real Greek music?'

He and his friend took me to a small flat near the covered market and put bazouki music on the gramophone. The sailor brewed strong coffee and brought sweet cakes and served them to us quite formally. Then he disappeared behind a screen and emerged with a piece of silver chiffon spangled with silver stars with which he danced.

Men, I learnt, are surprisingly good at striptease. When he had finished he put the screen around us. I fucked the arse off the Lieutenant and afterwards he asked me if all English boys had cocks like mine.

The two of them took me to a bar where their mates were dancing with each other and threw me into this scrum. I would have loved to have spent the night with them but had to get back to the YMCA.

GRAVITY

God declared that the earth was flat,
but Galileo put an end to that.
Eve's apple fell into Newton's bed,
Where a lad named Adam lost his head.

Newton's lad,
Bit the cox's pippin,
As he was strippin'.

Apple pie corners on Newton's bed,
Apple-cheeked Adam giving head.
Adam the apple of Isaac's eye,
Gravity's bent as apple pie.

NO BYRON

Lucca said the English had the most backward attitude to homosexuality in Europe. They were obsessed by it; an obsession that was theological, pre-scientific. This was all the more ironic as Isaac Newton, the founder of modern physics, was homosexual - he ate his apple with some bright lad. Nowadays, there is no voice that the oligarchy will listen to. No Byron. After fourteen years living in this country he said he no longer believed in our democracy, it was only the English who were under the illusion they lived in a free society. Whatever advantage they had in the past, the rest of the world had passed by.

An old and decadent oligarchy creaking under the weight of vacuous institutions - look at the monarchy puffed up by the stale air of the tabloids, the whole country is so awry. It is, he observed, Europe's madhouse, poor, derelict, and deprived; where the rulers batten on an ignorant and regressive working-class who are fed with the most tawdry material promises; so insular that no-one is able to see the shit-house this country has become.

What's left? Not even a theatre; the apology that has taken its place is populated by the middle-classes with their strangled vowels. No English man or woman could play Antony and Cleopatra; passion and love were quite beyond them, they could never discard their suburban subservience. Antony and Cleopatra would always be mere John and Norma.

HOW DAVIDE TURNED MY HEAD

In 1946, my father was posted to Italy. Overnight home was transformed from the bleak wartime married quarters with their coke stoves and mildew to a villa on Lake Maggiore.

Villa Zuassa had beautiful gardens. There I chased lizards among the enormous golden pumpkins that grew along the gravel paths, played hide-and-seek in alleys banked with camelias, or crept off to the gatehouse where a little old lady in the blackest mourning fed armies of silkworms on trays in the gloom of her front room. She would give me caterpillars and cocoons to take home, and I would be driven back through the woods by her grandson Davide on the handlebars of his bike. He would stop and hoist me on his shoulders to pick a particular flower.

Davide was my first love and the love was returned. He stripped off and rowed me on the lake as summer storms blew in from the mountains. This love was my great secret. If only this innocent idyll could have continued. But after a brief summer we left for Rome.

A VOICE-OVER FROM *CARAVAGGIO* 1985

Time stops for no man, not even the sun, said Pasqualone. My shadow passes. The flies spiral back.
Pasqualone yawns. Time stops for no man, he says caressing himself. I watch the ripples in his trousers.
'Can I put my hand in?' The words fall over themselves with embarassment. Pasqualone sighs and removes his hand slowly without looking at me. I kneel beside him and timidly reach into the dark. There are holes in his pockets. My hand slides in. His cock grows under my fingers.
Pasqualone says his girl Cecilia holds it harder, harder - the air hisses through the gap in his golden teeth.
Touch mine? Touch mine! But my mouth is dry and the words refuse to come. An ice-cold bead of sweat forms and trickles down my back. The seed is warm in my hand. His body tightens, he swallows.
'Harder, Michele, harder'. The words, violent and inaudible, fly round me, like the marble splinters in my father's workshop, stinging my cheek. Do it. Do it now.

THE SCHOOL SATCHEL

First sexual encounters have an arbitrary nature about them. Freddy told me that at sixteen, after school, he would cross the park in Richmond past the gents. One afternoon he was stopped by a policeman:
'What are you doing here son?'
Freddy blushed bright scarlet and mumbled some excuse.

'Don't let me catch you round here again, son.' The policeman took his school satchel from him and instructed him to meet him after school the next day at the station, when he would return it.

Freddy, terrified, arrived at the station where the policeman was waiting in a car wearing civilian clothes - 'Jump in,' he said, drove Freddy home and fucked him before giving him his satchel back.

In bed, many years later, Freddy told me it was the most exciting thing that had ever happened to him.

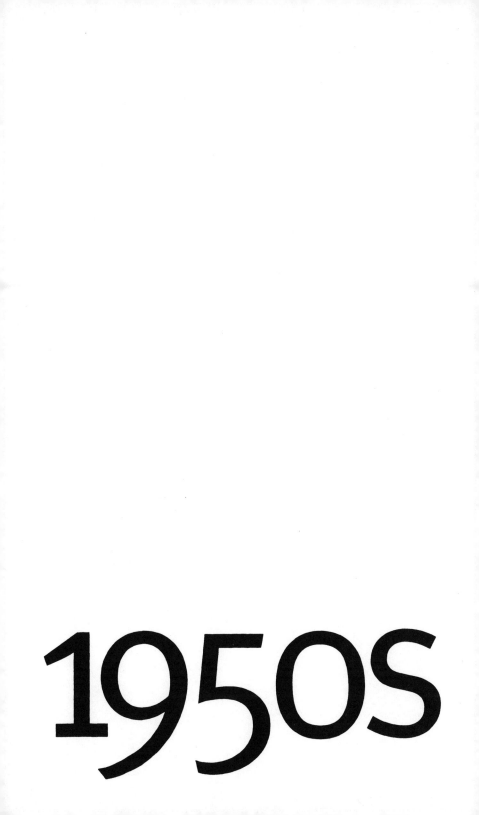

1950S

SCHOOLBOY 1950

I am a schoolboy with nine inches - meet me here tomorrow at 4:00 (Serious).

A schoolboy in a world imprisoned by Heterosoc. In prison, we are led to believe, no-one takes drugs, no-one fucks, no-one steals. Prison is the dream-world of Heterosoc, the desert of their Strangeways.

Heterosexuality isn't normal, it's just common.
Graffiti are the scratchy attempts by the sexually imprisoned to liberate themselves. They are pathetic remnants of a lost language of love, condemned to the walls of the toilet.
Graffiti, stammerings, they are always man to man.

A is for Antibody.
B is for Buggery.
C is for Crisis.
D is for Death.
E is for Everyone.

A 'system' of outward calm and apparent inner rectitude covered a cauldron of fear and resentment. The system's weapon was the bells which summoned us to grace, shrill and effective in penetrating the maze of corridors.

Laus domine. There were bells for lessons, bells for inspections of shoe polish, trouser crease, clean collar, combed hair. Punishment and beatings.

For what we are about to receive may the Lord make us truly thankful.

Bells for PT, the cadet corps, marching on the spot, field days, cross country running, rugby. There were character building bells, bells for fagging, above all there was the chapel bell.

Could all of this be conceivably thought 'a normal upbringing'? Everyone seemed to think so and my parents, bless them, paid for it. So much that my father proudly presented me with a complete set of receipts on my twenty-first.

Smarting under this tortured system, the boys tortured each other, imposed valueless rules and codes of conduct, obeyed imaginary hierarchies where accidents of origin and the caprice of nature were magnified.

SEX AT NINE 1951

I was aware of my sexuality at nine, which makes a nonsense of an age of consent of twenty-one and of the ideas of CONVERSION, PERVERSION and CORRUPTION of youth.

I was unsuccessfully trying to fuck the boy in the bed next to mine - quite unaware that I was doing anything out of the ordinary - when the sky fell in as we were ripped apart like two dogs by the headmaster's wife; and from that day and all the days of my childhood I waited in vain for a man to carry me off and initiate me - rescue me from suburban conformity.
   This happened to my schoolfriend Robin who had a wild affair that started on his fifteenth birthday - how I regret that I wasn't seduced.

Ian said he told his mother he was a homo at the age of five, and Jimmy told Michael that at twelve he was hanging around Glasgow bus station hoping some man would "shove it up him" - a youth intent on corrupting the middle-aged.

DESTROY THIS EVIL!
The Sunday Chronicle 1955

I cannot remember ever seeing an article in the British press which didn't see my sexuality in a negative light. Let us start in the cesspit of romantic fiction, and as you read this article know that in the fifties nearly everyone held these views. Have times changed?

Barbara Cartland writes:
   Our youth is menaced by these perverts, it is a sin against God and

mankind.

The irony was that these papers were kept out of our school in case they corrupted us! Now read on and you will see why...

This is an article a woman is supposed to be incapable of writing and an article which women should not read.

She went on:
It's topical! It's smart! It's modern! This disgusting sin against God and mankind. The majority have deliberately corrupted themselves and used every endeavour to corrupt others because, in their jaded and feckless lives there is nothing decent and nothing normal. Rigorous punishment combined with medical treatment is the cure.

Of law reform she said:
Nothing more sinister than this tolerance can be imagined. There must be a ruthless check-up on schoolteachers to check the hydra-headed monster of masculine perversion. Heaven knows how many boys have been permanently ruined by the ghouls of perverted sex.

Step forward the Duke of Kent and Lord Louis Mountbatten for dinner with Babs.

Sadly, Barbara Cartland was typical. Douglas Warth wrote in the *Sunday Pictorial* of: *evil men who thrive in the West End, a pestilence which is spreading to our provincial cities too.* He mentions law reform and says:
So many of these evil men go round corrupting youths and children. So many blackmail their victims who often enough are found in responsible positions. So many of them indulged in flagrant prostitution and commercial vice.

He quotes Clifford Allen, the psychiatrist: *these perversions cause a terrific amount of biological waste.*

This constant assault created trauma. One of the saddest tales I found whilst researching the fifties was of two young men from Haworth whose names I record. Lesley Smith, a fireman aged twenty-two, and his twenty-four year old lover Robert, a textile worker, who took a rifle and shot themselves. The headline reads: *FRIENDS FOUND SHOT ON BRONTE MOORS* and adds *they were quiet lads.* No romantic fiction in Haworth.

Years later in *Evangelical Times,* November 1986, Barry Napier writes: AIDS - JUST ANOTHER DISEASE? *To sympathise with unrepentant perverts is to condone their sin. We must love them as we must love any other lost sinner on his way to Hell.*

Why do the churches talk of love for the sinner when they forgot how to love centuries ago?

A SECOND INTRODUCTION

The prevailing attitude to homosexuals at the beginning of the sixties was a muddle derived from the church and psychiatrists: inverts, perverts, homosexuals, sodomites, inter Christianos non nominandum - not mentioned by Christians.

At best we were regarded with amused tolerance amongst the sophisticated, for the rest we were an abomination. Perversion was seen as an inherent and deep-rooted psychopathic state. It could, it was thought, be resisted - passions buried would not be awakened. It might even be cured by drugs, shock therapies, analysis.

Throughout the first years of the decade a moral crusade fuelled by the hostile attitude to homosexuals in the McCarthy show trials led to a spate of arrests culminating in the trial in 1953 of Edward Montagu - charged with 'serious offences' involving boy scouts. Among the most tragic losses was the mathematician Alan Turing, who broke the Nazi's Enigma code; he, as much as any individual, enabled the Allies to win the war. He was forced to take drug treatment to induce impotence, developed breasts, and committed suicide at the age of 41.

In the wake of these trials, the issue of law reform was raised in the Commons on 3rd December 1953 by the Conservative MP Robert Boothby to be scotched by the Home Secretary who insisted that homosexuals are, in general, 'exhibitionist and proselytisers' and 'a danger to others, especially the young'.

Forty years later all the old ground is being fought over. I have lived for fifty years as an unequal in this country, enveloped by hate; to ignore it I insulated myself, subtly changed my life.

No man is an island, but each man created his own island to cope with the prejudice and censure. The time for politeness had to end.

LOVERS' LANES

There are to be no lovers' lanes unless they are straight. Heterosoc is cutting down the trees. Clapham Common has been destroyed to stop us cruising. Friends are arrested in Russell Square and Holland Park.

I was put up against the wall there many years ago by a violent gang who I thought were out queerbashing. I was walking back home to Earl's Court from a showing of my film *Sebastian*, nothing more exciting, when I was jumped on. Only the fact that I was middle-class, white and had a film on at The Gate stopped a verbal assault - 'You fucking queer' - becoming physical. This gang were the police.

Now Heterosoc, if it can't destroy you, will destroy nature. They've cut down the glades of holly and cleared the undergrowth in Hampstead so that spring looked like a desert.

Nature abhors Heterosoc.
The wounded glades are healing.
Nature is Queer.

Hampstead Heath is in the news, the *Standard* has discovered an 'orgy bush'. You can buy these in the garden centre at Camden and plant them in your front garden. The orgy bush has beautiful red berries and is traditionally used to decorate your homes at Christmas to celebrate the birth of Jesus who loved John.

Heterosoc fuck in public on any hot day in Hyde Park near-naked without an eyebrow raised.

It is important to reclaim our sexuality from those who seek to sanitise its expression and weave it into the fabric of bourgeoise British morality.

MILFORD 1953

What is the world coming to when a peer of the realm can't bugger a commoner?

The trial of Edward Montagu from the *News Chronicle*:

> *A fourteen year old boy scout's account of a serious offence alleged against Lord Montagu of Beaulieu was described yesterday by a forensic expert as extraordinarily impossible. "I've studied the boy, he was strong, well built, and if there was any resistance this offence would have been impossible."*
>
> *Lord Montagu is the first peer of the realm to stand trial for felony before a judge and jury since the privilege of peerage was abolished in 1948.*
>
> *The fourteen year old boy was in the witness box for two and a quarter hours. The judge said that the boy's story had changed.*
>
> *"I wasn't sure, Sir." said the boy.*
>
> *"Are you sure now?"*
>
> *"Yes, Sir."*
>
> *"What made you change your mind?"*
>
> *"I don't know, Sir. I didn't know Lord Montagu was like this man as well. If you're in the presence of a Lord, one thinks you are fairly safe."*

My best friend Hugh lived with his parents in an old house next to Palace House in Beaulieu where the twenty-seven year old Lord had offered the fourteen year old a cigarette.

In 1953, I was eleven, and looked with excitement tinged with fear at the walls of the wicked palace.

The second case occurred when I was twelve. Edward Montagu was arrested at dawn in January 1954 with Peter Wildeblood who was later to write a fine book recommending reform.

There were nineteen charges concerning two young airmen. Pitt Rivers, the third accused, said: 'It's all part of this ridiculous witch hunt which is going on all over the country'. The case was tried in Winchester. Montagu got twelve months, the others eighteen but before sentence was passed Mr. Peter Rawlinson, for Wildeblood, called Dr. John Abbott-Hobson, consulting physician in the department of psychological medicine at Middlesex hospital.

Dr. Hobson said Wildeblood had been admitted to hospital shortly before the case so that his condition could be investigated, and also because there was a possibility of a suicidal risk. There was good chance of Wildeblood being cured if he remained under his care.

Mr. W. A. Fernley-Whitting-Stall QC, for Lord Montagu, said that had it not been for the recent events his client would be happily married.

The Judge said: 'I've paid the greatest attention to everything said on your behalf, but, of course, it's quite impossible for these offences to be passed over. I am dealing with you in the most lenient way I possibly can do'.

I was dimly aware that this national scandal related to me, though I had no words to describe it. 'Serious offence' related to what we called 'the lovely feeling'. After lights out, the boys jerked off in a competition to see who could come first - it makes you blind and saps the moral fibre and did you know it can make you grow hair on the palms of your hands?

Already the dormitory was divided into three groups: those who would report you - future guardians of morality; those who enjoyed themselves - myself; and the rest, frightened by their own come, and probably destined for the cloth.

WHY ARE YOU DOING THIS?

I don't have to talk film - they know I'm the film-maker, 'Good evening Derek'. I expected that this recognition might lead to aggression because some are not going to allow me the freedom to be on the Heath; but that never happened.

I saw a lad last night surrounded by four or five men. It was raining and terribly cold. He was giving them blow-jobs. He had a great physical beauty which distinguished him from those around him, though behind the looks they were probably the most gentle men. I picked him up off the ground. To my surprise instead of pulling away he complied with a sigh.

I put my arms around him. He offered me his last cigarette. Although I don't smoke I accepted it and walked with him. I wanted to walk right off the Heath and take him home, but I knew that wouldn't happen.

He told me a little about himself, just small things. First his name - which on the Heath is a big step. He was called Alex. He lived at King's Cross, and said he was going to meet his parents the next day - they lived somewhere north of Oxford.

I asked whether he was a student and he said no, he'd finished with all that.

He had dark hair, a soldier's haircut - short back and sides. He was probably 25 or a bit younger.

'Why are you up here?' I asked him.

'Well I can't sleep, I have to come up here sometimes, so I'm up here.'

'Well, I'm the same,' I replied.

I walked with him for five or six minutes, then gave him a hug. He said: 'To get to King's Cross I have to go back the way we've come'. I felt he wasn't going to do that but go back to giving those men blow-jobs.

Why can those who aren't here not believe that we who are can take responsible decisions about our sexuality? People have to take decisions for themselves. Even if he was throwing his life away, which is doubtful, it was a decision which he had made, no worse than going to war and dying for a belief.

Why are you doing this, Derek? I asked myself as I walked home. You shouldn't be out standing under these cold stars. You shouldn't have the stamina to do this. The answer was that I didn't have the stamina but throwing my arms around him was an act of defiance that kept me alive. Some shy from this sort of contact, from giving affection to a stranger.

For him the act was no longer limited by choice. It didn't matter who he loved. All those decisions that people make about their partners - they're acceptable, intelligent, bright - were all cast aside for something else. He was not making judgements. Where does judgement leave those who are excluded? This was a form of socialism, here was equality. I've always found that very attractive.

COLD BATHS

The threat of corruption, a dark sea of depravity lapped in the minds of the boys creeping up the very walls of the institution. The first sign of weakness was masturbation which blinded you on the football field and led to own-goals. Sex had to be turned off like the central heating. Outside the school grounds, the tabloids lurked in the shrubbery waiting to pounce on the naked men who locked you in their beach houses to perform their unspeakable perversions on your body.

Lectures on immorality would hold you in check, you beat your meat at the risk of expulsion and were dipped into ice-cold baths to toughen you up. Girls had crushes but boys had friendships. Crushes were sentimental. Guard against sentiment or they would find out your sissy heart. *They* lurked everywhere and even tramped across your dreams. Your whole body was a plague from the tips of your sweaty feet to the top of your spotty face. As puberty approached, frightful black hair sprouted, a dark forest to hide your embarrassment.

Meanwhile back at home, there were other randy airmen. My father, as C.O. of Abingdon, would never have known that Johnno, his batman, used to give me rides on his motorcycle round the married quarters, my hands in his pockets playing 'pocket billiards'.

SAVE QUEER CHILDREN FROM STRAIGHT PARENTS

In the fifties, sex education was non-existent and still is if you're Queer. At school, an elderly reprobate called Dr. Matthews came and lectured for three days with an epidiascope to the thirteen year olds, the fifteen year olds and the seventeen year olds. I remember him like the old quack, half medic half soothsayer, who performed to the crowned heads of Europe in *The Wizard of Oz*.

At thirteen years I was bemused by sperm projected thirty feet across. There was no emotional discussion whatsoever, sex was sex, the lectures were scientific, severely practical, limited and utterly heterosexual. Boys who had problems were invited to go and see him privately. One boy who wrote a love letter got expelled, so there was no likelihood of my going to see Dr. Matthews with my 'problem'.

My parents gave me a sex manual with lurid colour photographs. I discovered it in my bedroom and couldn't understand why it was there. I thought one of my friends had left it there, and was so embarrassed that I burnt it on a bonfire, as I thought my parents might stumble upon it.

There was never any discussion of sex in our home - this wasn't unusual at the time - so, as children we grew up in the dark, all our knowledge based on chance; chance, fate, and embarrassment.

Discussing the HIV infection with journalists I have found that few of them discussed sex with their children. They say 'oh my daughters are only thirteen', but many thirteen year olds are sexually active - just look at the figures for teenage pregnancies - so they *are* at risk. The age of consent should be lowered to fourteen or abolished and problems sorted out on an individual basis. We don't grow up to fit the laws.

So many kids lie about their age, as they are under threat if they are sleeping with an older man. I saw a letter recently from a sixteen year old boy which confirms this:
The whole concept of childhood is suspect. I was having sex at twelve. As a child I had no rights. I was seducing people in my school by the time I was thirteen.

A scenario for disaster! As a twelve year old you become HIV+, and then you fuck the whole school! The epidemic is potentially uncontrollable. The only solution is discussion rather than censure.

What do parents do?
I suggested to a friend that she bought condoms with her daughter and then discussed safer sex with her. It is the most responsible thing a parent could do. I see no reason why sex shouldn't be discussed with the very young. We start to talk about the birds and the bees when they're seven, why can't we talk about the birds and the bees and the condoms?

Did your straight friends let you near their children?
At first I didn't go near children. I couldn't be sure that their parents would know there was no risk. It was easier not to have to face that problem. There were so many other problems.

Did that hurt you?
Well, I wasn't in the habit of picking up babies - I wasn't a politician. I have few heterosexual friends - I became fed up being the spare man at their dinner parties. It's all right being Queer but if you talk about it everyone goes silent, everyone waits for you to stop.

This is why there is so much sex in this book - because that's what no-one wishes to discuss. It's important for us to talk about sex, to define ourselves in a world which has never talked about us or even let us talk about ourselves. If people can't understand that, they are very foolish. When you start to talk, it confirms you are living. If you are living under psychological terror what deals do you make with your oppressors? I am right to see it like that. This is the way it was and is, but not the way it was told.

Are straight people terrified of us because they see us chiefly as corrupters of children?
Their definition of corruption isn't realistic and, by their definition, we are corrupters of children. We always were; we wanted to tell children like it was, not like it was told. I was involved in the corruption of minors. That's why I made *Sebastian*. So that young men could have an option; the doors were opened into another world. I am certain that the world I live in is preferable to the one that my parents lived in.

NASCENT SEXUALITY

I have talked to many young men about their sexual experiences. One fact emerges quite clearly. Boys who've had the good fortune, at fourteen or fifteen or even earlier, to meet older men are nearly always more at ease with themselves sexually. The old Greek way of men and women initiating adolescents of their own sex, helping them to discover their own sexuality in an atmosphere of responsibility, contained much humane and practical wisdom. I'm unconvinced that any boy's 'natural' inclinations are ever altered by contacts of this kind. The only damage that can be inflicted is the threat of exposure by a 'morality' which outlaws innocent and uncomplicated desires, uproots affection at least as valuable as family ties, and affronts the basic freedoms of everyone.

WHEN I WAS YOUNG THE ABSENCE OF THE PAST WAS A TERROR

That's why I wrote autobiography. The *Gay Sunshine Interviews* in the seventies were important; it was the first time I had read interviews with men who were talking about their sexuality, very openly in the case of Allen Ginsberg - that thrilled me. In one of the madder moments last week I thought I might parcel up all my work, all my videos, and send them to him as thanks for the help he had given me when I was young.

In 1982, my friend Nicholas told me to write it 'out'. There wasn't much gay autobiography, some tentative beginnings in the gay press but no-one had written an autobiography in which they described a sex act - except Tom Driberg - certainly no-one in my generation. That seemed to be a good reason to fill in the blanks and to start putting in the 'I' rather than the 'they'; and having made the decision about the 'I' to show how things related to me so that I wasn't talking of others - *they* were doing *this* and *they* were doing that.

It was very important to find the 'I': *I* feel this, this happened to *me, I* did this. I wanted to read that. My obsession with biography is to find these 'I's. The subtext of my films have been the books, putting myself back into the picture. There's a huge self-censorship because we're terrified of betraying ourselves. We don't want people to know. Looking at historical figures and wondering: were they gay? They may have had the same sexual preferences but 'gay' is a late twentieth century concept. I always felt uncomfortable with it; it always seemed to me to exude a false optimism.

These names - gay, queer, homosexual are limiting. I would love to finish with them. We're going to have to decide which terms to use and where we use them. What about 'same sex relationships'? Maybe that's the best.

Yesterday Gore Vidal was talking about Noël Coward and managed to describe heterosexuality as a transgression! For me to use the word 'queer' is a liberation; it was a word that frightened me, but no longer.

What benefits are there bringing the past into the present?
Look at Tuke's paintings; they're pre-Freudian. Was he sleeping with these boys or was it that curious sanitised *Boy's Own* world of the Edwardians? Boy scouts and books with names like 'Five go on a Cruise'. An orgasm joins you to the past. Its timelessness becomes the brotherhood; the brethren are lovers; they extend the 'family'. I share that sexuality. It was then, is now and will be in the future.

I like the idea that we are linked in orgasm with Alcuin, St. Anselm or St. Aeldred, all of whom loved men physically. St. Aeldred wrote:

While I was still a schoolboy, the charm of my friends greatly captivated me, so that among the foibles and failings with which that age is fraught, my mind surrendered itself completely to emotion and devoted itself to love. Nothing seemed sweeter or more worthwhile than to love and to be loved.
 - *CORPUS CHRISTIANORUM*, HOSTE AND TALBOT - EDS.

Do you fantasize about these people sexually?
There was a night when I clicked into the ghost of one of my heroes, Caravaggio. It was an odd moment in which the past actually flashed into the present, physically - fucking with past if you like. I discovered my ancestry.

I wish I had been given instruction, both physically and mentally, by an older man. That is what teaching is about; it has to have a sexual element. That's what I like about Tuke. You can see he was in love with his boys. This doesn't have to manifest itself physically; celibacy can be very radical especially same-sex celibacy.

Do you see much of a barrier between the physical reality of sex and fantasy?
I think we play it out in public; sex is so codified. If you transgress Heterosoc you have to re-invent it. I have to invent myself in a way that my straight friends cannot imagine. I've heard of marriages where the partners haven't spoken for years but they still stay together. In the same-sex world if you stop speaking you'd split up. There's no reason why two

men who are not speaking should stick together unless they're trapped in property. Heterosoc is horrified by us because we are physical. Their denial of our lives leads to hate.

Do you think all men are homosexual?

Yes, all men are homosexual, some turn straight. It must be very odd to be a straight man because your sexuality is hopelessly defensive. It's like an ideal of racial purity.

50% of males who were interviewed by Kinsey had same-sex experiences at some point in their lives, not necessarily as teenagers. That was the old way of thinking: 'You'll grow out of it son'. A lot of them found it out later and it was very difficult for them; they were stuck in marriages, had children. As it wasn't easy for them to break out, they went to their clubs, played rugby football, immersed themselves in all-male environments.

And the army's not admitting Queers!

No, because they'd destroy its hierarchy. You couldn't have squaddies fucking with Major-Generals. The problem for straight men is that their sexual makeup is censored. The arse is an erogenous zone for all men, but whether they want to experience that is another matter.

At the beginning of the AIDS crisis, Dr. Joseph Sonnabend said that until you understood this you could not come to terms with the epidemic.

What about your attitude to masculinity? What does it mean to you?

I've never really defined myself as masculine.

There's a curious piece in Dancing Ledge *when you say:* Until I'd enjoyed being fucked I had not reached balanced manhood. When you overcome your fear you understand that gender has its own prison. When I meet heterosexual men I know they have experienced only half of love.

Because as an unreconstructed man you had to be in control. It is about control. If you aren't the dominant partner in the sex act then you are emasculated, you are unsexed. It took a long time for me to realise the falsity of that. 'He's uptight, tight arsed': you've got all these colloquial expressions about anal sex. It's difficult to overcome that conditioning.

Within the gay community there was a heavy emphasis on who was 'butch' and who was 'bitch'. It was to counter that that I wrote about being fucked rather than fucking in *Dancing Ledge* and it worked the way I thought it would - in some reviews I discovered myself being described as 'unmanly'.

You will still find people playing roles but it's a long time since I went into a bar or club in London where people talked in this way - 'Oh look he's butch', '(s)he's bitch/femme'. As one loses potency in old age it's easier to get fucked than have to fuck.

This might be another reason for the elderly and rich employing rent boys who they perceive as tough.

WOLFENDEN

On Wednesday 4th September 1957, Sir John Wolfenden's committee completed its report on homosexual offences and prostitution. None of the fifteen members were homosexual, nor was any homosexual consulted. A few weeks later, on 26th November, the commons debated the report. Sexual acts in private between consenting adults over twenty-one should no longer be a criminal offence. George Monro wrote for The *Daily Herald* under the headline *Men Without Women:* 'Homosexuals are harmless biological misfits. I've been investigating this most delicate yet frightening problem. It's unlikely the government will accept the main recommendations on homosexuality.'

He was right. It would be nearly ten years before the laws were changed.

General Kitching of the Salvation Army said: 'few would dispute that homosexuals are inimical to the social, moral and spiritual welfare of the country and degrade human dignity'.

Kenneth Younger MP (Labour) said, 'the existing laws made a mockery of justice', but he added, 'I do not know whether homosexuality will become less socially harmful if the consent between adults becomes law'.

I was sixteen. Public statements like these gave no comfort as, legal or illegal, I was a problem to these people, maladjusted and socially harmful. At the end of the *Herald* article I learnt that in Moscow they solved the problem by putting us in prisons and concentration camps. The concentration camps were in our minds; they didn't need to be a reality.

Throughout the year the report was debated. In the *Scotsman*, Graham Turner wrote, 'the church has a major part to play in fighting the evil of homosexuality'. He suggests that teams of 'thoroughly trained moral welfare workers' should be formed. He reports talking to a psychiatrist: 'we have to find a way of life attractive enough to deter them from yielding to compulsive urges. I believe there is nobody more fitted than the church to meet these needs' - a thought I find as ridiculous as lions helping Christians with their spiritual problems. Dr. Davidson, a minister, said: 'Why did we spend so much time in romanticising perversion? The answer lay in the power of the holy spirit'. He added, 'if the church was to play a real part in helping the homosexual, it must first win back his confidence. Homosexuals found by the police could be cautioned and then sent to a moral welfare worker which the church might appoint. If homosexuals could be brought into communion with a fixed body of normal people, such as one meets in a Christian community, a very great step will have been taken. This would be a very distinctive Scottish contribution to the problem.'

In another article for the *Scotsman*, 'Control Must Come Before Cure', Turner says, 'as one Glasgow psychiatrist told me, the usual treatment is to administer some drugs'.

ONE LAST LOOK AROUND THE FIFTIES

I was first aware of my sexuality at nine, but I was very isolated. If only I had met someone who could have helped me through my adolescence. I had one schoolfriend who had the fortune (he's now married with four kids!) to have a long affair with a schoolteacher. This affair continued right until his mid-twenties.

I was abducted by Heterosoc. When I was thirteen, I changed schools; the next school, if anything, was more violent about sex. It is a myth that all-male boarding schools are the centre of jolly sexual activity. I remember putting my hands down a boy's trouser pockets and touching him up, but that's all. I might have surreptitiously brought him to orgasm but I can't remember.

One schoolboy was hauled up in front of the headmaster for writing a love letter to another boy, he was expelled. Love was a worse crime than sex.

I had sexual fantasies about some of the boys. There was one night when two of the boys retired under a bed in the dormitory. I'm not sure what they were up to. I hardly dared look. The rowdiest heterosexual boys were able to have these homosexual encounters, whereas the Queer boys were frightened because it was the centre of our sexuality. We didn't dare make the advance.

All the way through school I had hopeless crushes. I was bullied mercilessly, I wasn't interested in the school agenda and it's pluses and minuses.

I knew I wanted to paint very early on - painting was my secret garden. My art was an escape out of Heterosoc. The art school was separate from the main school buildings, so I could lock myself in there. I would win all the art prizes, that was my validation. It used to upset the other kids.

Like a lot of young men I was afraid of my body. I don't think this is to do with my sexuality. I was terrified of changing rooms and physical sports, and I came in for a lot of aggression because of that.

I've remained angry about it ever since and, because it made me desperately unhappy as an adolescent, it's one of the motivating forces in what I've done with my life. Adolescence is difficult enough for any of us, but to have those pressures on top of it, to be corrupted into heterosexuality, that was the worst.

The atmosphere in a school like that in the fifties would horrify people now. I can assure you the winds of change didn't blow as far as Dorset.

Was there a tyranny?

There was, and is, a tyranny. A lot of abuse and ridicule about cocks in school.

Did your parents ever talk with you about your sexuality?

No, they knew instinctively, but there wasn't any way of talking about it then; and by the time I was grown up, there didn't seem any point. I guarded my sexuality against them although I brought my boyfriends home and they stayed. My mother was welcoming. She worried about me. She didn't want me to be unhappy.

My father frightened me. It wasn't just the incipient violence. He always had this belt round his neck and it was as likely to come thrashing out of the blue sky as... There is no escape from parents, you're stuck with them. It was so bad my mother sent me for holidays with my grandmother. I would spend hours in Watford milling around junk shops in order not to be at home.

Did you ever seek comfort in religion?

No, my parents were agnostic. My mother sent the priest packing on her death bed, she said she wasn't a believer. My father hadn't time, he was always sailing.

I became interested in religion as an art student. I studied art history and iconography and I found it fascinating. Later I studied church history to try and find out why the church cannot look life in the face. I had to come to terms with that tradition or fight it.

For the same reason, Pasolini made his film *The Gospel* - a generation before me. His situation was more repressive than mine. It makes me sad that his sexuality was strangled in the shadows. On the other hand, his struggle with this is what makes his art so vibrant.

ARE THERE ANY PARENTS WITH THEIR EYES OPEN?

At nine, I was caught in bed with Gavin - thrown onto the floor by the headmaster's wife, lectured publicly and whipped. Frightened by this unexpected outburst, I was to have no physical contact for thirteen years. I lived my adolescence so demoralised I became reclusive. The physicality of sport, particularly the changing rooms, were an agony of deception. I was desperate to avoid being the sissy of my father's criticism, terrified of being the Queer in the dormitory.

I was most at ease with our matron. I painted pictures for her living room, vague copies of Van Gogh blossom. My work also suffered. I dropped behind. At puberty my reports said 'more concentration needed'. You see I was distracted.

WEDNESDAY 27TH NOVEMBER 1991

OutRage! demonstrated outside a school handing out positive information to the pupils. The newspapers are full of indignant politicians, parents and schoolchildren. The negativity of the response shows how important this action is. No-one is Queer at Haverstock School: they would be too frightened to identify themselves to the journalists. Instead we have kids saying 'I don't agree with them protesting as heterosexuals don't protest like this' or 'as long as they keep their distance, they can do what they want to do'.

The first thing that has to be acknowleded is that we are you, there is no distance. We are forced unwillingly to accept Heterosoc and you are our misfortune. Silence puts the young in peril. Heterosexuals have really nothing to protest about. Their fundamental being is not under assault twenty-four hours a day. Let them tinker with the niceties of their family lives but recognise that our relationships are not validated, which is a transgression of human rights.

According to a study by Exeter University, there are six and a half million of us under assault in this country alone.

In 1990, over 14,000 calls were made to the National AIDS Helpline by lesbian, gay or bisexual children under the age of sixteen. A further 38,000 came from lesbian, gay or bisexual young adults between the ages of sixteen and twenty-one. If these figures show a degree of anxiety amongst young adults and children what about the fears of children that are left unrecorded? There is little discussion or even less research about homosexuality in childhood.

In 1984, a survey of about 400 gay teenagers in London revealed:

38% felt isolated.
32% had been verbally abused.
19% had been physically assaulted.

As a child I was in all three catagories. It's no wonder that 19% of gay teenagers attempt suicide. Gay teenagers are 2 - 3 times more likely to suicide and comprise up to 30% of suicides annually (US Department of Health statistics). Are there any parents out there with their ears open?

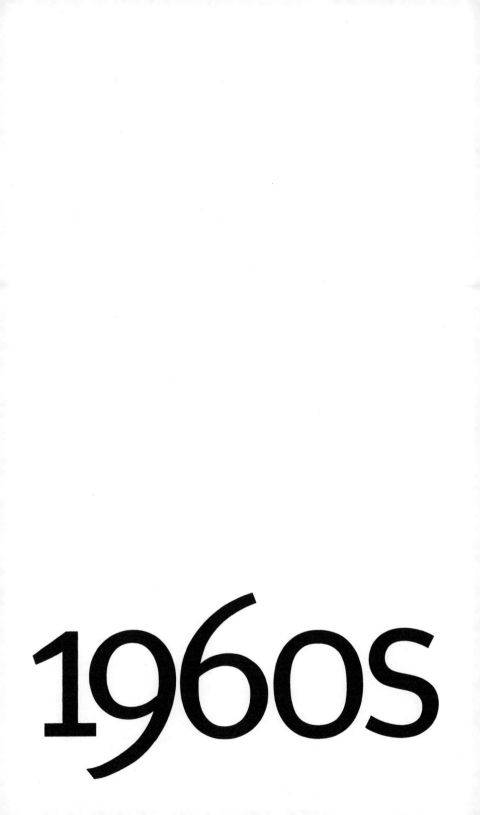

1960s

KING'S COLLEGE - LONDON 1960

Eighteen years old. No gaysoc or anything like that. There was one identifiable Queer, Stuart, who I got to know after I left the college. He was much too sophisticated for the students. He worked in the first John Stevens' in Carnaby Street during his summer vacation, and came back wearing outrageous red pants with which he embarrassed the theologians (King's was a theological college) and fascinated the rugby players in the refectory.

One of these, a lad with straw-blond hair, very well built, used to hang around at lunchtime in his sweaty sports clothes. I'd wait for him, hoping he might talk to me, but, terrified he might spot my interest, I didn't so much as smile at him. Each night I returned to suburban Northwood where I had a girlfriend who was also at King's. In those days she wore outrageous fifties dresses with organza petticoats which stuck out horizontally like the singer Alma Cogan's.

Years later, I met her with her girlfriend at Winter Pride.

There was no life in Northwood other than the most restricted manifestations of Heterosoc, Conservative dances, and nights out drinking in The Truelover's Knot. Home was over an hour on the train from college in The Strand so I hardly got involved in college life; all I remember is the endless travelling with City gents in bowlers hidden behind their newspapers. I didn't know anyone I could stay a night in London with and made no attempt to, terrified that I might have to share a bed.

Nothing changed until I moved to Coram Street near Russell Square at the age of twenty-one. In that year I told Roger, one of the theologians, I thought I might be Queer. He reacted in a very affirmative way but had no solution. 'I've heard there are people like that. Don't worry, I think I met someone like that in New York.' There was nothing much to go by. It seems ludicrous now but information was non-existent. Even if I had dared to, I wouldn't have picked up the Wolfenden Report to find out about my life.

HOW, IF I HAD DARED, I WOULD HAVE HATED YOU

The repression was difficult to confront - like finding your way down a foggy street. In the sixties, we were to be open but illegal. This did not make it easy to form relationships and led to fumbling, furtive sex. There was little or no celebration until the end of the decade, although things were getting better. It might seem that our sex lives were anonymous, but you'd be mistaken if you believed that.

I remember the name of every boy I slept with in the sixties, even if it was for one night. These encounters took place in bedsits in an atmosphere of frustration. Long bus rides, and when you were there, shellshocked inability to love. Tortuous, stilted conversation until you got to the point. It was the Americans, at the end of the decade, who said 'Hi, let's fuck!'

Heterosoc kept its tabs on me; my parents were still alive. Would they murder me, exile me, what *would* they do if they found their son was a 'pervert'? There were few young people in the bars, only the old who had come to terms with their *fate*.

There was no way of judging a boy's sexuality, so I fell hopelessly for straight boys on motorcycles. Hours in the company of Mike Snowball, a dark-haired, blue-eyed hunk of an architect; or Lawrence, who thought he was Jimmy Dean, axle grease all over his faded blue Levis, who crashed his bike with me riding pillion.

I eventually realised this love of straight men was futile but the lads I liked were not in the Queer pubs. All I looked for really was a sparkle in the eyes. I wasn't fixated on genitalia and I would have been horrified if I thought that was the only attraction.

I was into 'higher' things: plainchant, the modern movement, great poetry and plays. It's true that our generation missed out on itself. None of us lived with each other, the time was against it.

In the past if you had met another man you would live with him for life, but that didn't happen often, so all the Queers got married. That world was ending; a long sleep was ending and we were the dazed first generation through the door. I read *The Allegory of Love* and decided I was not part of the romantic tradition which had been pulped into cheap novels.

I was modern.

When I came to the University, I was unaware of Queer bars and clubs. I wasn't to meet anyone until I was twenty-one who admitted he was Queer and he was as old as my father. I didn't tell him of my feelings - I didn't dare. I was another young man corrupted and co-opted by hetero-sexuality, my mind still swimming about in the cesspit which is known as family life, subjected to a Christian love whose ugliness would shatter a mirror. I had to destroy my inheritance to face you and love you.

AT A LONDON ART SCHOOL - 1964

There was no language or discourse that I could relate to, nothing. If I'd seen the Wolfenden Report in a newspaper at that time, I would have hidden it, or quickly turned to the next page so that no-one thought that I was reading it. My life was snarled up.

That same year, I met my schoolfriend Roger and his girlfriend Brenda. Roger had a long affair at school with an older man, Michael, and now they all shared a flat in Camden Town. Michael's open homo-sexuality seemed very strange to me. He would sit and play the piano in this basement all day, singing bright songs of buggery. 'I know you're a Queer, come on Derek, admit it'. 'No, no, no!' I said, scarlet with embar-rassment.

It was there that the crisis occurred. It was a crisis.
One evening in March, I went round early and Michael wasn't there; a young Canadian was sitting at the piano. He was a student of psychology at Alberta University. We were the same age, 22.

I missed the last bus and Brenda said to me, 'Why don't you stay in Michael's bed tonight, it's very late and he's not coming home'. As I was falling asleep Ron crossed the room and got into bed with me. It was so unexpected. I didn't acquaint Queer people with youth. I thought they were middle-aged as the papers said.

When Ron got into bed, I was so startled I just lay in his arms. Next morning when I awoke, he'd gone. Were we going to see him in the evening? 'Yes', Brenda said, 'he's going to come back'. I thought - shall I ring him? Better not, I'll wait.

I wandered aimlessly round London - couldn't face going to work at the Slade. That evening we had all been invited to a party in a flat behind the Middlesex Hospital by one of Brenda's friends; Ron never appeared. In my panic I consumed a whole bottle of whisky. I was carried home, almost unconscious.

The next day, Ron still didn't appear. I was in a terrible state. He was the only Queer lad in the world. A blind rage of self-destruction overtook me. Roger had always collected my paintings; they were all over the flat. I took Brenda's dress-making scissors and threatened suicide. Fortunately I didn't harm myself but the whole household was in turmoil as I carved into these paintings - it's quite difficult to hack a painting to pieces. Brenda was in tears, Roger quite ashen-faced. They tracked Ron down and brought him over. This time he stayed.

The next morning I took him to Northwood to meet my parents. We stayed the night there and decided to hitchhike to Somerset. We got as far as Slough. It was raining and we just couldn't get a lift. I looked at him and said, 'Why the fuck am I taking you to the West Country? Why don't we go to Italy?' So we went back home, picked up some clothes and took off. We couldn't sleep together as we were staying in Youth Hostels.

Two weeks later, when we got back from this escapade, it was obvious to both of us that we were Queer as hell, so Michael danced a polka on his piano and said to me: 'Right, none of this shilly-shallying, we're all going to the 'Willy' in Hampstead'. I was horrified at the thought of going to a Queer pub, but there was safety in numbers.

The William IVth was thoroughly middle-aged: elderly models and artistic antique dealers. There was one marvellous man with 'blond' hair who must have been all of seventy. There were artistic ladies, all of whom had modelled and fallen in love with Stanley Spencer. On my second visit to the William IVth, I met a young man who was as new to all of this as I. He had a bright red MG sports car and was working in advertising. We decided to explore London after I returned from the States in the autumn.

There was no music in the pubs. It would be wonderful if there were one or two places as quiet now. There were very few young people 'out' -

mostly old queens who'd sat at the bar for years on end hoping that some 'chicken' would come in - and when we did we were totally uninterested in them. They bubbled with anger behind the rouge.

I thought I was an ugly duckling, but in fact, looking at the old photos, I was the dish they'd been waiting for. I wasn't having any of the coffee lark: 'Would you like to come back to my place for a cup of coffee, dear?' The idea that a cup of coffee was an invitation to bed surprised me.

Daphne, Stanley Spencer's mistress, was the Queen of the place. She took me under her wing. I was rather frightened of her; I think she wanted more than a peck on the cheek. Stanley had lived with her *and* his wife for years in the same house. She had great art stories for a young painter like myself.

GREEK TO ME - 5TH FEBRUARY 1963

All BBC television and radio announcers have been instructed that in future the word 'homosexual' must be pronounced 'hommo-sexual'. The instruction came from the Corporation's pronunciation department. It explains that the word derives from the Greek root meaning same, and not from the Latin 'homo' meaning man. The BBC say that the directive was issued to clear any misunderstanding on the pronunciation of the word. No-one really knew how to pronounce it properly.

Heterosexuality: what is it? how is it caused?

James Lindesay writes:
   Heterosexuality (derived from the Greek 'heteros' meaning different, rather than the Latin 'heitare' meaning 'to yawn') is a condition in which the individual is sexually attracted to members of the opposite sex. It is becoming increasingly apparent that heterosexuals (or 'drabs' as they call themselves) do in fact make up a significant proportion of the community.

FROM A BOOK OF MICHELANGELO'S SONNETS I BOUGHT IN 1962

And if the vulgar and malignant crowd
misunderstand the love with which we're blessed,
it's worth is not affected in the least,
our faith and honest love can still feel proud.

ART ACTION

It may seem ludicrous now that stumbling on Marlowe's outing speech from *Edward II* could be an eye-opener. His list of Queers included Socrates and Alcibiades. The Greeks knew how to live. Sappho and Plato were a revelation. In his *Symposium,* Plato recommends that only young men who love each other are fit for public office.

I began to read between the lines of history. The hunt was on for forebears who validated my existence. Was Western civilisation Queer? The Renaissance certainly was. Lorenzo di Medici, Michelangelo, Leonardo, Botticelli, Rosso, Pontormo, Caravaggio, Shakespeare, Marlowe, Bacon.
Music was less Queer - unless it was British in which case it was absolutely Queer - but there was unhappy Tchaikovsky forced to suicide by the evil Tzar because he was having an affair with a young aristocrat; the writers Whitman, Wilde, Gide, Proust and James. By the end of my first year at college I'd acquired some heavyweight soulmates.

Most of the works on our Queer lives underestimate the effect of art in favour of political action; I think this is wrong. I know that my world at eighteen wasn't the the gift of politicians but of the identifiable homos; Cocteau (above board), Genet (under the counter), Burroughs and Ginsberg (heard of but not read). In 1962, we performed Genet's *The Maids* at the college. It caused as much fuss as a political action might today.
The sixties were to see major interventions by artists. David Hockney publicly acknowledging his sexuality from the beginning of his career; Kenneth Anger and Maya Deren's gift of the underground cinema; feature films like *Il Mare;* Andy Warhol's sexual circus; Rudolph Nureyev's

leap to freedom.

What did that mean to me or my friends with cock up our arses and come splattering the ceilings? We joined THE UNDERGROUND. The underground, like the bars, was illicit. In the theatre the Lord Chamberlain was tight-arsed, no homos, and homos of eight or eighteen unthinkable. The theatre of the angry young men: DEAD STRAIGHT - the theatre was of *no* interest. Film was more interesting; at the first showing of Anger's *Scorpio Rising* and *Fireworks* at Camberwell art school we expected a police raid. The theatre reduced us to a load of laughable pantomime drag queens; it was in painting that the leap forward into normality was made in *We Two Boys Together Clinging* by David Hockney, and later the startling reality of lads I knew or recognised in bed together in the *Cavafy Etchings*. Books travelled easily, Burrough's *Naked Lunch* and Ginsberg's *Howl* finally purchased.

Leap ahead 20 years to the mid-eighties and the scarcity of information in the 'Soviet Union' of Heterosoc had changed. For a twenty year old unaware of the details of his continuing illegality there were Andy Bell and Jimmy Somerville to fuck to, novels from the Gay Men's Press, photos by Mapplethorpe, and Weber, film, theatre and the freebie press.

Weighed against this were the old moral proscriptions, reinforced by years of deliberate misinformation in the AIDS scare; put out by government and press aided and abetted by people like Victoria Gillick - the professional Catholic - and Mary Whitehouse's flirtation with the corpse of nineteenth century morality.

AMERICA 1964

At the end of the summer term I went to the States on a British University Club flight. I was one of the first of my generation to get to NYC. My friend at King's who had said, 'There's not much to worry about Derek, there are lots of people like you in the world', gave me the address of some priests in North Henry Street.

Manhattan was still a port in those days, nothing like now. Imagine *Querelle* Stateside; there were ships, sailors, truckers and meat trucks.

Everything's been cleaned up since. I don't know where you would go now to find that atmosphere. Barcelona? Marseilles? It was both frightening and exciting.

My air ticket gave me one night in an hotel called the Knickerbocker in a room the size of a pocket handkerchief with eight other young men trying to sleep on a ferociously hot July night.

The next day I met Roger's friend, the priest at the Episcopalian Centre. In the taxi he tried to get his hands in my pants. This was the first time anything like that had happened and it threw me.

His friends were really tough: sweatshirts, frayed jeans, black crosses, crewcuts and scars. That night in the mission, these priests tried to fuck me, but I wasn't having it. I had never had anal sex; that didn't happen till much later. I was hardly aware it was possible. They ended up jerking off all around me. Of course, I was flattered by all the attention - a sort of priestly gang-bang.

Next morning, they took me to a church which they called Mary on the Verge, high Episcopalian with all the altar boys winking at the congregation. I couldn't fit it into anything I had previously experienced. Shortly after, I took off on the greyhound bus for Canada and Ron, wondering what the hell I had got myself into. I wrote bad poetry on the bus all the way, dreadful stuff.

Manhattan

Now I have seen
screaming manhattan
thrusting to burst bounds
crush the sky
and wade into cool waters
I have seen
serpent taxis
jewly gemming
winding through stainless steel corsets
narcissistically reflecting
and scratching the sky
I have walked through
lives littering the lower east side

dominoes with death
and the rat crumbling
furnaces of july dwellings
dreaming of time-sapped Europe
now I have ridden subways at 100 mph
elevators 40 storeys a minute
glittered in the electric wastes of
park avenue
rode the staten island ferry
and watched this city
recede like a kodak dream

'Now I've seen Manhattan!' In Calgary, I had Ron's parents to cope with - they were unaware of our relationship, totally unsuspecting. They couldn't afford to look after a third person so I got myself a job on a city survey measuring the slaughter-houses. Wading around in blood and gore. Ron and I started to quarrel - it must have been difficult for him. God, he was glamorous. He had a job as a lifeguard, so while I was staggering around in the slaughter yards he was standing by his swimming pool in white.

Late in the afternoon after my daily bloodbath we'd have a swim, fool around in the pool; it was great fun but we didn't have sex. The rows got worse and I took off South for San Francisco, hung about the City Lights bookshop where I bought a copy of *Naked Lunch,* and all the Allen Ginsberg poems, a library I had to lug around in my rucksack. I thought I would be arrested at customs - these books were banned back home.

Hitchhiking up the coast I met a young man on a motorbike who took me to the Hell's Angels' convention at Monterey. He rolled joints all the way; it was the first time I had taken illegal substances. We met the organisers of a Joan Baez concert raising money to stop Barry Goldwater winning the Presidential election. At the end of the concert she said, 'I have my friend, Bob Dylan, in the audience'. The audience went crazy and Bob Dylan came and ground out 36 verses of a ballad before we all went to a party in Cannery Row. Can you imagine the effect all this had on me?

I went back to NY on the bus. It took three days and nights. When I got there I rang up the reverends. I decided I was going to stay with the least obnoxious of them. He said to come round. I was exhausted; I hadn't slept for two days.

'We're going to a party!' he said.

'Oh God, I'm so tired.' It was a Queer party and racially mixed. Half the party-goers were in drag. They were all camping it up. I had never seen anything like it. There was a competition to find who was the best 'woman' in the room, a battle between the black drag queens and the white drag queens that turned quite nasty. Really vicious!

A black boy who was as embarrassed as I came over, grabbed me and took me into the bedroom where all the coats were. We had sex. It was the first real sex I'd had. The drag queens got very angry; we had locked the door and were fucking on their coats.

Afterwards we couldn't find my reverend anywhere so I presumed that he'd gone home. We walked back to his place but he hadn't returned and, as we were locked out, we curled up in front of his door in each other's arms.

Much later he came back and found us asleep like that. He was scandalised. He shouted at us. Then he went inside, got my rucksack and threw it out - my clothes thrown all over the place, my books and passport, and shouted 'Fuck off! - What do you think you are doing?' My new friend, Marshall, put me back on the plane to England that afternoon.

You said that everything up to that point had been a prelude...

Yes I did, this boy was sexually experienced. He knew what he was up to. We made love.

Did you come back Queer?

Definitely - and with crabs! The sex I had with Marshall wasn't penetrative, just mutual masturbation. At that time there was great to-do in the gay bars. It was almost automatic e.g. 'do you take it?', 'do you give it?'. All the camp lingo, the double (and single) entendres. Because of the repressed situation in which people lived, a private language was created. Michael was continuously ragging me, saying, 'You're not a man until you've been fucked, Derek'.

How did you cope coming back Queer? You'd slept with a black guy, you'd got into the Beat scene, you come back to Britain and...

I went straight back to my parents' house in Northwood. I didn't know what crabs were. I remember scratching and thinking, 'God I've got fleas!' I was so naïve. I told my mum: 'I've picked up some awful creepy crawlies'. 'Oh,' she said, 'I wonder what those are?' and sent me to the family doctor. My father remained silent; he must have known what these bloody insects were but he didn't say anything at all.

The doctor said, 'Now let me just see'. He picked up an enormous book and leafed through it ponderously - maybe he didn't know what they were! Had crabs ever been seen in middle-class Northwood? After a long pause he said, 'Ah yes, these are lice. Have you been sleeping with prostitutes, Derek?'

I was dumbstruck. I thought I'd better say yes. He said, 'Well, you'll have to mend your ways'. He gave me a prescription for mercury fulminate - the most ancient Victorian remedy. I went back home and sploshed this all over myself. I remember my mum laughing and telling all her friends 'Derek's got nits!'

GOING TO A CLAP CLINIC - 1965

My friend Richard was the first of us to go to a clap clinic at University College Hospital where he discovered he had syphilis. The irony was he had had only one lover. His discovery threw me into turmoil as I decided whether or not I dared to be tested.

I finally got the courage together and found out I was clear, but I well remember walking backwards and forwards along Gower Street uncertain where the entrance to the clinic was - as it was hidden in the basement and difficult to find.

I went into the main entrance and, after what seemed an age, asked the receptionist. 'Oh, you want the *special* clinic' she said. So, keeping an eagle eye open, in case any of the students at the Slade across the road saw me, I rushed down the stairs. The experience left me quaking.

I MEET THE HOMINTERN

I met David Hockney one cold autumn day at the Picasso exhibition in the Tate Gallery. I'd gone with my friend Ossie who made the fashions for all the stars of the sixties. David, had come straight to the gallery from the airport; he invited us back to his home, a large, cluttered flat in Ladbroke Grove. It was so cold we got into bed fully dressed while he brewed tea and unpacked a small suitcase which was full of *Physique* magazines and bright fluorescent socks. Everything about David was a delight, his mismatched socks in acid green and lemon, the bright shock of dyed-blonde hair, his pink jacket and his deadpan northern wit. Ossie and he were old friends from Bradford.

The sparsity of his luggage surprised me. Only ten years before my parents had travelled to Pakistan with cabin trunks and porters; and the journey, through the Suez Canal, had taken three weeks. Now you could hop on a jet and buy your toothbrush and toothpaste at the other end.

Through David and his friend Patrick Proctor I met all the young painters; this changed my life. There were shows and parties and nights on the town; we all fell in and out of each other's beds. It was enriching. Sex was bonding, pedagogic, a way of learning.

PUBS AND CLUBS

There were a handful of clubs if that. The Gigolo which was underneath a fashionable restaurant in the King's Road; The Casserole, owned by a man who had the flat above which was hung with Francis Bacons - very good ones, maybe eight in all.

A narrow staircase led straight down onto a red-tiled dance floor at the most 15 feet square, probably less; the place was painted white. There was a bar where you could only get Coke and Nescafé as none of the clubs were licenced. That's why drugs came along; you couldn't go out for a weekend on Nescafé.

At the back was a raised area - about 10 feet square - with two toilets off. Most London bars were similar. Music as far as I can remember came from the jukebox.

We weren't allowed to touch when dancing. If you touched anyone the doorman would say, 'Hey lads, come on, you know the rules'.

At the back of The Gigolo everyone had their flies undone. It was jam-packed. The management turned a blind eye to this. At the bar people would be balancing their glass cups of Nescafé, chatting about art! There were more young people in these bars than there were in pubs.

The bars were still on the edge of legality. The police were likely to raid and they did. During a raid pretty policemen would mark who had touched them up, then arrest them on the spot. Upstairs, you were searched again. I had to walk home all the way to West Hampstead from the King's Road. There weren't any night buses. London was ill-served in that way.

La Douce in D'Arblay Street, Soho was different: less middle-class, mod boys, and a smattering of rent, and you could stay into the early hours. It was the most exciting club of the sixties and it was where the 'hip' hung out - dressed in John Stevens (the difference between clothes then and now was cost - Carnaby Street, which set the style, was cheap). Elastic-sided Chelsea boots, bright trousers and shirts swept away a grey past. Even Levis jeans were new - all those lads sitting in tepid baths to shrink-wrap their arses and a little sandpaper round the crotch to show off a packet; they shouldn't be too tight, or your partner couldn't get his hand down the back and dance with his fingers stroking your arse when no-one was looking. Jeans were sexy - if you came in them they could be washed - and they were good for cruising. Anywhere where men were out for sex they wore jeans - and still do.

Unlike The Gigolo, where you might find yourself blown in a dark corner, the La Douce was rather straight, the sort of place you might take the more adventurous mum for an evening on the town. It did not close its doors until the sun was up, and played good music. Downstairs there was a small dancefloor and a seating area screened off by a tank of tropical fish. I don't remember the lads picking each other up in the La Douce with the ease they developed later, it was a place to dance and socialise.

People who hadn't got anywhere to go when it closed would get themselves breakfast in a greasy, all-night café and then go to sleep it off in the Biograph Cinema - a fleapit in Victoria. The Biograph showed 'dodgy' films like *The History of the Body* or, now and again, a Pasolini film, and the most dreadful German *Health and Efficiency* films with girls in leather pants, topless, holding steins of beer.

The straight mackintosh brigade hung out there. It was a mix; you could make a real mistake if you put your hand on the wrong crotch. He might be a drunken tramp who'd start shouting and swearing - 'fooking queers!' - and then fall into the aisle! By this time the whole cinema would be in uproar and the old ushers would staggering around with their torches like searchlights at the height of a bombing raid.

The rules were strict: to change seats so you could sit next to someone you fancied you walked up the aisle to the toilet which was right up against the screen. The old men with torches would flash them and throw you out if you disobeyed this unwritten law.

The Biograph was run by the brother of the boxer Henry Cooper, with an eccentric old lady at the door - there were always mad old ladies at the doors of cinemas! That's changed.

I don't wish to give the impression that we were out every night - perhaps once a month. My painter friends were not ardent clubbers.

What sort of people did you meet in the bars?

I met one young man who topped David Hockney's blonde. He had dyed every strand of his hair a different colour: silver, pink, green, blue and mauve. Once he came to the Slade for lunch wearing a smart business suit and rolled umbrella and turned every head; he was a 'happening'.

I was lucky if I had sex. Everything was more difficult. There was still a large amount of restraint on my part.

The first time I had sex in London was with an actor. He was about thirty. I went round to see him after he finished work and fucked him - that was the first time *that* had ever happened as well. I didn't fancy him particularly, but he was good at it when push came to shove.

The whole decade passed quite innocently. There were few distractions; the sub-culture had not taken off. All the clubs were owned by semi-criminals. There were restaurants which were Queer, run by camp Spanish queens in very tight trousers and pink frilly shirts; I was put off by them - I was searching for a regular lad.

I once had a wild stand off with a theatre queen, Michael Weald, known as 'Minnie' to his friends. One summer's evening at The Colville in the King's Road, he invited me home to a party. When I arrived at his flat, he closed the door and locked it, taking me into his huge sitting room which looked like the set for *Spartacus* - enormous, black leather sofas wallowing in white shag-pile like hippopotami, watched by marble busts of wall-eyed Roman bankers on tall plinths.

Minnie Weald appeared thirty seconds later wearing only a silk dressing gown, a pudgy pink prawn, darting about his drinks cabinet. He fixed me a brimming tumbler of neat spirits and slid onto the sofa beside me.

I cowered into the corner as his cobra hand darted out and hovered over my crotch. I slid up onto the arm of the sofa, 'I wonder when the other guests will get here. It's getting terribly late. I think I better go before the tube closes!'

'Don't worry,' lisped Minnie, 'you can stay, I've more than enough room!'

By this time, I'm in the hall struggling with the locked door. Minnie bears down on me, I duck and bolt back into the living room seizing one of those antique, marble bankers which rocks ominously. 'Don't, don't!' shrieks Minnie and rushes to unlock the door.

I stumbled out into the night... I'd missed the fucking tube.

PICCADILLY POLARI

BONA EEK, DEAR! We had our secret language. VADA THE RIAHS! The turn of the cuff, the handkerchief in the back pocket, the ring on the little finger of a BONA PALONE so we could recognise each other on the streets.

The modern Queer was invented by Tennessee Williams. Brando in blue jeans, sneakers, white T-shirt and leather jacket. When you saw that, you knew they were available.

There was nothing more exciting than a stranger stopping and looking back and the chase ending in front of a shop window, mirrored in the glass; the long journey to his place or yours; cocks throbbing and minds racing. Slipping him out of his jeans and sucking his cock, the ecstatic kiss, the discovered tattoo. Wild as a boy can be, sparkling eyes, laughter, the taste of him, the sudden mad rush to orgasm after hours on a tightrope of sensation.

STRANGE CLUB - DAILY MIRROR, FEBRUARY 1963

Scenes from a club where men dance with men are to be shown on BBC television. A camera crew from the Panorama *programme has visited the club which is run for both men and women homosexuals. It is called The Link and is in a side street in the centre of Amsterdam. The Link is licenced by the police under Dutch law. 'The BBC understood that our club members would not like to be filmed dancing so they didn't even suggest it,' said a member of the club.*

BBC SHELVES FILM ON CLUB -
DAILY MIRROR, MAY 1963

'At the moment, I don't think we could put it out. It doesn't make a self-contained story and it would raise an issue if it went out at the normal Panorama *time.'*

Since the British could never face themselves, it was unthinkable there could be such clubs in London so they located them elsewhere, on the continent. I remember the TV cameras coming down to La Douce in 1967 when the law had been changed. Everyone afraid to be filmed and at the same time, desperate the film should be made. I was one of those who didn't go that night, worried that my parents might see me on the television.

THE KING'S ROAD

The King's Road changed rapidly through the sixties. When I first walked down it it was still a high street with bread shops, paper shops, cafés, and a sprinkling of art and antique shops. Chelsea grew as a working-class annex to Kensington and Belgravia; colonised by artists: Wilde, Turner, Whistler, and many others. I don't think artists lived there by the sixties.

The Colville, now a clothes shop, was the most visible of our pubs, opposite the barracks. Further down The Queen's Head for the indigenous Bohemia. The Casserole and The Gigolo - fashion and sleaze. The Gigolo

- in The Basement - was small and dingy but one of the best known bars of the sixties. The Casserole was above a fashionable restaurant - with the Saturday afternoon promenaders. Across the street, Vern Lambert held fort in the Chelsea antique market with one of the first and best second hand clothes shops, specialising in silk scarves from the thirties that no pop star in 1967 could be without.

Next to The Casserole a new club opened, The Hustler, again a small basement but it sported a décor - a motorbike fixed to the end wall. Yet further down the road, past the World's End, was The Place, so crammed on a Saturday night you couldn't move. The King's Road clubs were definitely up-market, all closed by 2am.

The 19 bus returning north after the pubs closed was a riot. The old graveyard, now a park, became a meeting place on warm summer's nights, and the undergrowth provided cover for sex. The fire station had a 'reputation'; it was rumoured that the firemen constructed a swimming pool, and bathed naked, locker room stuff. A lucky Queer wandering home in the small hours might be invited in to freshen up and give them head.

Swinging London swung in the imagination rather than reality; however, there was a limitless horizon of optimism. What were these bars like? None of them would pass muster these days; apart from the lack of alcohol, sound systems were in their infancy so dance floors were an afterthought.

The Gigolo with its steep staircase was probably a deathtrap. Certainly panic set in when the police raided. People were arrested more by bad luck than design. You waited your turn to be frisked and given a numbered piece of paper which you showed at the door upstairs before you were allowed home. After the police left the floor was a sea of recreational drugs jettisoned in the dark.

These raids carried on right into the seventies - they were designed to frighten us, stop the less adventurous leaving their homes. The Gigolo was visited by all the well-known Queers about town even if infrequently: Nureyev, Hockney, all those who gave London the illusion of glamour. Pop stars like Bowie, and Mick and Bianca Jagger would join in later in

Kensington when the Sombrero opened its doors.

THEATRE QUEENS

If you didn't go to bars and clubs, where else was there to meet? Well, if you were Joe Orton you cruised the 'cottages', as the theatre, historically the meeting place of queens, was so fucking polite. Radical in their politics and conservative in their lives, the Royal Court their strip. British actors and directors threw parties which were a welcome alternative from the pubs.

Tony Richardson's were the wildest. He invited me to his house in the South of France in 1968. All the young painters were there; David Hockney photographing boys nude in the swimming pool.

Tony's obituary in the *Standard* gave the wrong impression suggesting that he was leading a double life - he was completely open about his sexuality.

Many of the young danced at these parties; in the absence of today's sophisticated bars, gallery and theatre openings were important for us.

At Hockney's '68 Kasmin opening a friend - the painter Steven Buckley - said 'Well, you're running out of Knights to sleep with, Derek' very loudly. I had just finished designing Frederick Ashton's *Jazz Calendar* and was in the middle of *Don Giovanni* for Gielgud. Fred Ashton, who was meant to hear this (and did) laughed.

After Gielgud's parties in Cowley Street broke up I was propositioned by taxi drivers summoned to take me home to Islington. The Queer cabbies staked out the stately homos; as they dropped me off said, 'Aren't you going to invite us in for a cup of coffee?'

A POP-UP NAZI POPS UP

The blackest sheep of the art world was Sir Francis Rose. Old art commies crossed the road when they saw him coming, with his shock of silver hair, huge ring and corkscrew walking stick.

In the mind of Gertrude Stein Francis had been in competition with

Picasso to be the world's greatest artist. He was the Rose of her famous aphorism 'A Rose is a Rose is a Rose'. Sir Francis, once as rich as Croesus, had fallen on hard times. He was now virtually a tramp though prevented from falling into complete destitution by his friend Cecil Beaton.

Francis had taken a wrong turning somewhere in the thirties, perhaps because he was not only the premier Scottish baronet but also a grandee of Spain and therefore hobnobbing with General Franco and taking holidays with Hitler in his Bavarian mountain retreat.

I have been fascinated by Francis ever since Southwark police delivered him to my studio in a black maria at four in the morning; he had turned himself in whilst on the run from Wales, where he had been stoning the stained glass windows of a parish church.

At a GLF meeting a few years later he hissed at me, 'What we need is *real* men not all these fairies, Derek'.

In Paris during the war, Francis had been telephoned by Marshall Goering - another of his dodgy friends. Hermann had heard that Francis knew a famous fortune teller who we shall call Madame Sosostris. The Führer, who was deeply superstitious, wanted a reading. Francis and Madame met the Marshall in his sky blue uniform and, I suspect, his fishnet stockings. The message he got for Hitler was 'You will find your fortune in the East!' The next day Adolf ordered the invasion of Russia. So Francis indirectly was responsible for winning the war - and the death of millions.

When I last saw him, I found him painting pop art pictures of old Nazis. I made the terrible mistake of saying I found the paintings 'interesting'. He turned round and said darkly, 'One's friends are always interesting, Derek'.

THE MEN APART - EVENING CHRONICLE, 1965

The man in the chair in the blacked-out room is a homosexual. There is a projection screen before him. On it flashes a picture of a male model with a fine physique. Seconds later, as the photograph lingers on the screen, an electric shock races through the body of the watcher. As the sensation passes, the picture of the male is replaced by the image of an attractive woman. The sequence is repeated again and again and again. The image of the man is thus linked with displeasure and that of the female with pleasure. This is a brief summary of a form of treatment for homosexuality known as aversion therapy. In a way it is frontier medicine. It will be years before anyone can say quite definitely whether it is successful or not.

The man who was subjected to this assault was probably arrested 'cottaging' - meeting men in a public toilet. Outside London it was this or nothing. Most towns had, at best, a dreary pub. This is still the case if you live in a small town or village. The 'cottage' is the foundation of our historical lives. It was here that we were condemned to meet by Heterosoc - which fought the opening of the bars, their minds, and anything that might suggest we led normal lives.

BRITISH MEDICAL JOURNAL, 1965

Many regard the excess of male deviants as evidence of the operation of a biological factor. Affected persons are commonly of late birth and commonly born to older mothers. No abnormal chromosomes have been detected. Studies have emphasised the defective parent: demanding over protective, seductive and inhibiting mothers and negative hostile fathers.

The very close relationship of homosexuality with the other sexual neuroses is also in my experience borne out by the very marked deficiency of the tender emotions and the altruistic sentiments in all these conditions - most marked perhaps in homosexuality - so that these sufferers are deprived of the enormous stimulus which the tender emotions normally contribute to the sexual instinct.

SOME OF MY BEST FRIENDS ARE

It eventually dawned on me that heterosexuality is an abnormal psychopathic state composed of unhappy men and women whose arrested emotions, finding no natural outlet, condemned them to each other and lives lacking warmth and human compassion.

Deviant heterosexuals are the product of sympathetic, warm and over-protective fathers, and cold distant mothers. Whatever the cause, aversion therapy was probably their only chance. Like all compassionate Queers, I knew heterosexuals needed help desperately. How could they be saved from themselves? Perhaps a nice clerical counsellor sponsored by the Church of England.

I was young and insecure. I might have been handsome and bright but I was not in love with myself. I had come from a boarding school where I was bullied. This made me introspective. I tried to cover up, I built defences against the world. I think that will remain with me for life.

If someone had dropped me in Old Compton Street when I came to London in 1960 I wouldn't have known where I was, I was so green. I didn't have much to say, nothing to say about sex. I was tongue-tied - the tongue-tied boy. What I didn't know is that youth has its own attraction. When you're young you don't realise that. There are very few young men who are unattractive. It would be good for them to know that, to have the confidence I lacked.

What I would wish is for a generation that can come to terms with itself quickly, not have to go through the struggle my generation went through to accept ourselves. We had a bravado that wasn't backed up by experience. I met up with a group of people who were active in changing things; that was my fortune. It gave me a comradeship to deal with life.

My parents didn't want me to become a painter. In the fifties people couldn't live by painting; it was considered a hobby. My parents would have said 'Derek's hobby is painting'.

I was pushed off to university where I had a broad education in History, English, History of Art and Imperial History - I took that because it was such an unpopular subject and it interested me to go to a class where all the students were politically suspect.

THE 19 BUS STORY

It was one of the most exciting nights. I had nowhere of my own to stay, but my friend Karl had lent me his flat above the Shaftesbury Theatre.

I got off the 19 bus at Centrepoint, there was a jeweller's shop there and I saw a young, very sexy guy, looking in the shop window. He caught me looking at him and shouted at me very aggressively: 'What are you fucking looking at?'

It really shocked me, I wasn't expecting it and it was obvious that I had been staring at him. I didn't reply, didn't want to end up knocked to the floor. I crossed the road to go down to Karl's flat, walking with my back to him, thinking I'm not going to look.

Suddenly there was a piercing wolf-whistle. I turned round and he was on the other side of the road further back, waving at me to come over. He gave another loud whistle, so interest overcame hesitation. As I walked back, I remember I kept a distinct gap between us in case he lashed out at me.

'You got a problem, you queer or something?' he said.

'Yes, I am.'

'Can I speak to you?'

'Yes, but I'm not interested in having a fight over it. If that's what you want pick on someone else.'

'No, no, I want to speak to you'.

So, rather awkwardly we walked down the road; I was thinking I'm not going to take him up to the flat. Can I trust him? There's no-one there. So we walked around the Shaftesbury Theatre.

In those days a magazine shop with soft porn was there. We stopped to look. He said, 'Have you got any magazines or anything?' 'Well, yes I have' - they weren't mine, they were Karl's. Karl was leading a wild life at that time, much more crazy than mine, he was fixated with rugby players and footballers and had a huge stash of magazines in his room which had a tideline of KY round the wall. I had never collected magazines. I liked looking at them, but for me they were never a substitute for the real thing.

I took him into the bedroom and threw him a pile of hard core gay magazines, then went into the kitchen and made coffee. When I came back he was engrossed. Before we'd even sipped the coffee he had his pants down; I fucked him all round the room and he came over the magazines.

After it was all over, he said, 'I've never done that before'.

He told me he was a plumber's mate and wrote poetry. He was really handsome. I thought he was beautiful, but as I gave him the address and phone number and said, 'I'd really like to see your poetry', I knew that I would never see him again.

LAW REFORM - 4TH JULY 1967

The bitterly disputed bill was finally passed into law. Esmond Knight reported in the *News of the World*:

Leo Abse's bill on homosexuality legalises homosexual practises between consenting adults providing the adults are both over twenty-one and the acts are carried out in private.

The bill had its vigorous opponents like Rear Admiral Giles who spoke out against a 'queers' charter' and stressed that it would be seen abroad as further evidence of Britain's degeneration. 'It would,' he said, 'encourage our enemies and dismay our friends'.

The *Standard* reported that:

Opposition crumbled early this morning during another marathon all-night commons sitting. Opponents had fought to the bitter end. Fears that the bill would lead to the establishment of private buggery clubs for the enjoyment and promotion of homosexual activities were voiced by one MP. Mr. Peter Mahon (Labour) opposed the bill "lock, stock and barrel, root and branch, hook, line and sinker, warts and all. It was by no means unnatural to have a feeling of absolute revulsion of a bill of this type, it was bad to begin with, it was a bad bill now and it would be a bad bill to the end of time".

The *Daily Mirror* wrote: *At 5:50am BST after a night of dubious jokes and personal clashes, a social revolution begins.*

DID YOU EVER KNOW A NICER BOY?

It never struck me that relationships were necessary. I never thought of them; they seemed to be something my parents' friends had, most unsuccessfully. My parents' marriage was happy enough, but my father had no adventures simply because of middle-class propriety, nothing else. Was there anything to emulate in these relationships? What was the point of them?

In my world, I met different people and exchanged ideas, it never occurred to me that anyone would want a settled relationship. Of course, some of my friends had long relationships, but was that an advantage?

Relationships have come much later in life for me, but I've never regretted the fact that I did not fall in love at that time. I had a series of firm friends instead. I was a bit of an adventurer. By the end of the sixties I was living in derelict warehouses, which was a far-cry from people who were getting mortgages in Islington. I never felt they were doing the wrong thing, why should they think I was? Everyone I knew, knew everyone else, and everyone I knew had slept with everyone else. We all lived together as a generation, not as a family.

Talking of families, one of the strangest encounters that I heard of was from a friend of mine, Gawain, who picked up a young man, who introduced him to his brothers and his father. The father was sleeping with his sons and the sons were sleeping with each other and Gawain and his boyfriend were asked to join in! They shared a holiday and an enormous communal bed. Everyone was very happy.

My life had fluidity and possibility. There were more casualties in Heterosoc though one friend of mine starved himself to death for love - he became anorexic and died. But people were no more likely to go mad in a bar in Soho than they were in Epsom at a point-to-point. When that happened we tried to help; sometimes we were successful, sometimes we weren't.

What was so exciting was meeting new people with new ideas while Heterosoc felt that all we were doing was putting cocks in each other's mouths. Before those cocks got into our mouths we were exchanging ideas.

I'm not looking back unhappily because of what happened later. All of these relationships were life-affirming. I would lead that sort of life again at a drop of a condom!

So many of these people remained lifelong friends, often the ones that I met in what might seem the most extreme circumstance. We're still in contact; they're only a bar away.

We spent our time jettisoning fears and phobias and *they* spent their time acquiring them, whoever *they* were; John Junor, Geoffrey Dickinson and Alexander Walker. I feel sorry for them because they must have had such impoverished lives.

OLD MORALITIES, NEW LIFESTYLES

The fifties witnessed the post-war break-up of the old social constraints under the assault of American consumerism. Sex before marriage had became commonplace, not the exception.

On the surface the old morality still held. The sixties were infatuated with the Bloomsbury group, upper-class Bohemians who led open and ambisexual lifestyles in the twenties and thirties. A reaction to the First World War, in which the dominant male sent thousands to their deaths.

We were smothered with information about the Bloomsbury artists. It wasn't to do with their work, more to do with their love life - Virginia Woolf was bisexual, Vita Sackville West had a lesbian affair, Maynard Keynes was queer, so was Strachey who had my friend Robert read him *Gentlemen Prefer Blondes* in a Paris hotel one night.

There was a spate of biographies. The lives of the upper-classes were being popularised. This broke the secrecy that surrounded us and we pitted ourselves against the old moralities. We were no longer sick; even American psychiatry was to decide that in 1972.

We outed ourselves from the closet, got out on the streets and demonstrated. We would come up with new ways of living. Our lifestyle became *the* lifestyle; *we* set the styles for youth culture.

We were economically more independent than our parents. There was an emphasis on youth, clubs, and all of the paraphernalia of popular culture. Things changed rapidly.

The sixties liberated us. When the lights were out the boys dropped their pants. The fifties had been the 'low dishonest decade', not the happy time of the haircut-which-everyone-adopted-in-the-eighties, the silly pottery or the ghastly furniture shaped like painter's palettes. They were quite different. The West End went East for rough trade. There were much greater social divisions.

It's no wonder that a generation in reaction should generate an orgy, it came as an antidote to repression. Heterosoc - because it controlled the media - would congratulate itself on its morals, its monogamy, and use this against us. It was all very well for the police to raid a 'rotting' sauna and for that to be reported in the press, but the sauna was there because of the oppression.

THE PEACE OF ANONYMITY - STONEWALL WAS A RIOT

The queers of the sixties, like those since, have connived with their repression under a veneer of respectability. Good mannered city queens in suits and pinstripes, so busy establishing themselves, were useless at changing anything.

To be Queer was never respectable - even though you wore a suit. The more conventional, the more desperate a hidden life. Pushed to the fringes, our world existed in the twilight of Heterosoc; that was the reality, and if anyone raised their voice in protest they were accused of endangering the peace of anonymity. A demonstration was likely to frighten the closeted, their inactivity reproached.

Stonewall was a RIOT which occurred in the summer of 1969 in Christopher Street, New York outside a bar of the same name. For the first time Queers fought back with bricks and bottles and empty beer glasses and burned cars. The best fighters were the trannies - a dress was the badge of courage. This riot sparked a revolution in our consciousness. A community of interest was established and a debate was entered. The harder it was fought the more our case was furthered.

Everything that made our world visible reproached the closeted. One day it might be as silly as moaning about Quentin Crisp's blue rinse as a BAD ROLE MODEL, or, on another, complaining of a rowdy Gay Liberation Front meeting. For them, we were not them. They took everything and did nothing, sat in their interior decoration, attended the opera and did fuck all to help change; their minds as starched as their shirts.

Twenty years later, Stonewall - the self-elected and self-congratulating parliamentary lobby group - have made more than enough compromise with convention. Did those who rioted at the Stonewall bar fight so that we could so easily be co-opted by a gay establishment? Do they represent our best interests in Heterosoc?

Do they represent us?

Why did one man go to Downing Street to put our case? Why were there no women? Weren't the rest of us acceptable? It was as if no Queer had ever been in number 10 before, the fuss everyone made.

When Mrs. Thatcher met the British cinema to find out its problems, she saw a spectrum of people from Richard Attenborough to Isaac Julien. All of them spoke. Was lone McKellen's visit an election ploy? Gay votes would make the difference between a Tory or Labour government; we are at *least* one in ten of the population.

Was McKellen representing only himself as he maintained? If so, it wasn't seen that way. At the last general election a poll in the gay press showed that support was evenly divided between the political parties, but who could vote Tory after Section 28?

Perhaps you could if you could accept honours from them. Honours support a dishonourable social structure. Barbara Cartland, Ian McKellen and James Anderton; there's no merit there. To have accepted them showed a terrible vanity. And there's our only 'out' gay MP (Labour) crawling in this sycophantic trough, criticising me in the press. All the hard work put in by activists for a different world - not the same old world - was betrayed at this moment.

McKellen is a charming and intelligent man and that's the problem. Oh, the shark has pearly teeth, dear, with eighteen minnows following. One of them, Schlesinger, is making promos for the Conservative Party; the party that ruined the eighties and made our lives hell.

Part of the con was to steal the name Stonewall and turn *our* riot into *their* tea party. We are now to be integrated into the worst form of British hetero politic - the closed room, the gentlemen's club - where decisions are made undemocratically for an ignorant population which enjoys its emasculation.

So they - Stonewall - won't acknowledge this criticism. They'll pretend there isn't a debate. The only way that they can succeed in their politics is through the myth of homogeneity and the 'gay community'. But our lives are plural. They always have been - sexuality is a diversity. Every orgasm brings its own liberty.

AS THE DECADE ENDED

Much had changed since that night in March 1964 when I kissed Ron. Now I was dancing at my own party to end the sixties in a warehouse on the banks of the Thames.

Johnny had spent a week putting together a tape of all the great hits of the decade and we printed an invitation that was given to all our friends and handed out to the best looking lads on the King's Road.

Wayne's T-shirt which proclaimed 'To live is to dance and to dance is to live' said it. By midnight, the studio was packed and the party had spilled out into the street where Ossie rolled endless joints and the police stood idly by as they believed royalty was present - in fact that wasn't the case though Tennessee Williams arrived at one o'clock with a group of handsome bodyguards.

As I lay on the sofa at four in the morning, I could hardly believe the change that six years had brought. Ron had kissed me, Marshall caressed me, Jack took me to bed, Tom had me fuck him.

At nine the next morning, there were still fifty or so exhausted revellers when I called time and shut the doors. The next decade would bring the wild boys you dream about and an unexpected meeting with a film student that would change my life; but on that night I could not have known this.

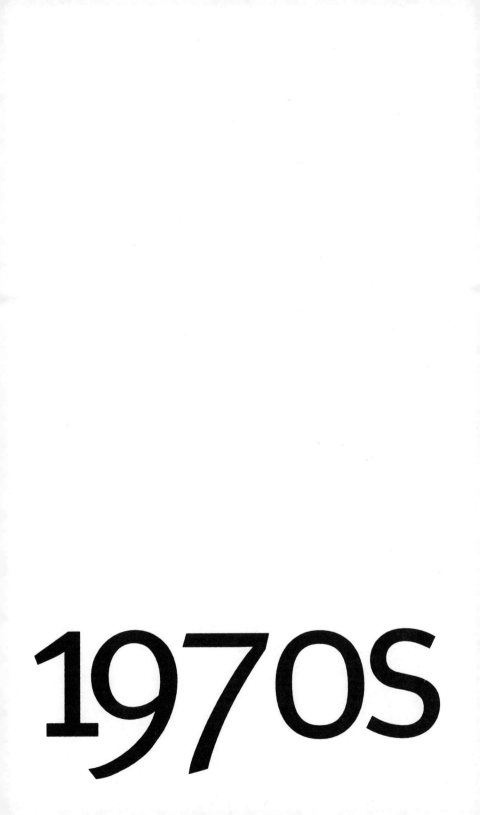

1970S

GAY POLITICS AND THE FOUNDING OF
THE GAY LIBERATION FRONT

And now we're all GAY!

GLF was formed in the autumn of 1970, ten years after I came to London. It had been preceded by other groups, the most successful of which had been CHE, whose members were not young art students and for us represented a different world. I danced the sixties away but I didn't see that as hedonism; it was a REVOLUTIONARY GESTURE - you should have seen the way the other students reacted to two men kissing in public. I believed we could bring change with individual actions, it wasn't linked to any conventional political blueprint. One person in one room quite cut off could change the world.

Political events looked like hated school photographs. Even GLF at times could take on the appearance of Leonardo's dreadful picture of the Last Supper. Christianity with its altars and congregations replicated itself in a thousand secular manifestations.

The GLF meetings in the lecture theatre at the LSE were electric; there must have been a hundred or more people there. I sat on the edge of my seat as the debates were hijacked to protest about Vietnam. They veered all over the place but at their centre was the idea of 'coming out' and 'gay pride'.

I wanted to speak up but this was a younger generation. The speeches were so fiery I couldn't have competed. I've never been able to speak in public - if I'm asked a question I can answer it; but make a speech, impossible.

My revolt against authority was instinctive. I could not be a subtle diplomat; I'd rather sink the ship of state than just rock the boat. Though to shout too loud I thought, might make me foolish and I didn't want to appear foolish.

After the meetings - which seemed chaotic through lack of restraint on the part of the speakers - there were demonstrations, and dances attended by hundreds of us. I loved these events, lurked in the shadows, an observer, unquestioned.

I knew things were wrong, less certain why and not certain how they could be changed. For me, GLF became a place to cruise as well as a place to learn. The GLF was sexy; everyone was 'out'; it had action and celebration.

I still feel that there is no sexual liberation unless it's personal. Struggle to find out who you are. It's no good joining a group and making speeches about what you want to be, life is to be lived first and proselytised after. I was in full revolt against life as it was lead by most of my fellow citizens. I couldn't bear them. I could see nothing of any value in Heterosoc, in marriage, mortgages or family.

I was young and attractive and everyone was after my arse. The appalling claustrophobia of Heterosoc could be subverted there.

In the next few years, our culture grew out of GLF: *Gay News*, Gay Sweatshop theatre group, Gay Switchboard - which answered calls for help and acted as an information service, Gay's the Word bookshop and Gay Men's Press.

GAY LIBERATION FRONT MANIFESTO, 1971

The GLF manifesto outlined our oppressions under a series of headings: family, school, church, the media, words, employment, the law, psychiatry; and ended with a piece on self-oppression. These are a few extracts.

FAMILY
The fact that gay people notice they are different from other men and women in the family situation causes them to feel ashamed, guilty and failures. How many of us have really dared be honest with our parents? How many of us have been thrown out of home? How many of us have been pressured into marriage, sent to psychiatrists, frightened into sexual inertia, ostracised, banned, emotionally destroyed - all by our parents?

SCHOOL
In the context of education, homosexuality is generally ignored, even where we know it exists, as in history and literature. Even sex educa-

tion, which has been considered a new liberal dynamic of secondary schooling, proves to be little more than an extension of Christian morality. Homosexuality is again either ignored, or attacked with moralistic warnings and condemnations. The adolescent recognising his or her homosexuality might feel totally alone in the world, or a pathologically sick wreck.

CHURCH

Gay people have been attacked as abominable and sinful since the beginning of both Judaism and Christianity, and even if today the Church is playing down these strictures on homosexuality, its new ideology is that gay people are pathetic objects for sympathy.

THE MEDIA

Under different circumstances, the media might not be weapons of a small minority. The present controllers are therefore dedicated defenders of things as they stand. Accordingly, the images of people which they transmit in their pictures and words do not subvert, but support society's image of 'normal' man and woman. It follows that we are characterised as scandalous, obscene perverts; as rampant, wild sex-monsters; as pathetic, doomed and compulsive degenerates; while the truth is blanketed under a conspiracy of silence.

WORDS

Anti-homosexual morality and ideology, at every level of society, manifest themselves in a special vocabulary for denigrating gay people. There is abuse like 'pansy', 'fairy', 'lesbo' to hurl at men and women who can't or won't fit into stereotyped preconceptions. There are words like 'sick', 'bent' and 'neurotic' for destroying the credence of gay people. But there are no positive words.

THE BRADFORD ZAP

GLF took to the streets and invaded the British Medical Association congress on psycho-sexual problems.

Further explanation and reassurance with encouragement to control [the homosexual's] fantasy life and make heterosexual contacts... cases with strong uncontrollable and undesirable sexual urges which can be damped down by giving oestrogens or one of the newer anti-androgen drugs. Certain limited forms of brain surgery are still in the experimental stage and only a very few cases have been reported.

-BMA *FAMILY DOCTOR PAMPHLET*, 1973

The zap was effective in highlighting the appalling record of medicine and psychiatry in our lives. It was reported widely under headlines like *Gay Lib Storm Stage At Sex Congress* and *Doctors At Sea In Gay Lib Demo.* The news was being made by us not about us. Fifty hissing, heckling members of GLF invaded the hall for over two hours and brought the congress to an end. Activist Don Milligan, wearing a sequined dress, told the delegates: 'We don't like the way you talk about us as aberrant'. A victory, the end of psychiatric interference in our lives, was about to be won.

NINETEEN SEVENTY

In 1970, I moved into a warehouse on Bankside, next to Southwark bridge. I made my first small film of the studio on Super 8. I was absent for much of the year building sets in Pinewood Studios for Ken Russell's film *The Devils.* The film studios were violently heterosexual and I realised quickly that I would never work in the British cinema; it was so contrary to my life, a return to a world which I had mercifully begun to forget. Up at six-thirty, back by ten, no time for bars and boys. It didn't matter that many of the actors were gay. Our lives there were closeted. The studios were hierarchical, and our sexuality was betrayed by the cinema.

My warehouse gave me space. My hair grew longer, my jeans were scattered with diamonds so they shimmered in the night, my ear was pierced and I wore extravagant earrings, not little gold sleepers; I had rings on my fingers - big ones - bright yellow plastic boots, and tie-dyed shirts.

The boys I loved were no longer English: Raul was a Brazilian, Serge was Russian and Gerard was French, the grandson of the great actress Falconetti. Life was cosmopolitan.

I received good advice from an older generation - the painter Robert Medley and the choreographer Fredrick Ashton. I took problems to them and they spoke their minds. In Bankside, I slept on a sea of cushions in a greenhouse which I covered with luminous stars. Below me, the Thames reflected light onto the ceiling.

Dawn came up at Bankside on acid.

URBAN GLAMOUR ASSAULT 1972

A shopping trip. Trying on a floral bathing hat in the women's department of Derry & Toms in Kensington, I was attacked by the floor manager who, in a tornado of abuse, shouted right across the room, 'You there, get out!' I was admiring myself in the mirror.

Andrew Logan had invited me to his Alternative Miss World party, the Ascot of radical drag. The hat really did look good on me and I had always loved dressing up.

The whole place went silent. 'Get out! You hear me? We don't serve your type in here.' Now she stood before me shaking with fury. To my utter surprise I stood my ground without a blush. I was determined to have this hat; it had taken me the whole fucking morning to track one down for the swimwear section.

'I want to BUY the hat, I'm not just trying this on for fun. This is serious.'

'It's not for sale. Get out before I call the store detective.'

'Well, it's got a price tag on it and it was in the sale.'

'NO, NO, NO!'

Then I did what you always do in the movies; I asked to see the manager.

'He won't see you.' she said.

Up on the sixth floor, I pushed my way into the manager's office. He looked rather startled.

'I want to make a complaint,' I said, 'I was in the women's department trying to buy a bathing hat and was thrown out by the floor manager.'

'Weren't you in the wrong department, sir?' He said this with terrible respect.

'No,' I said. There was silence. 'I was buying clothes for a huge drag ball in Ken Russell's new film. We were going to spend thousands here. I'm his designer.' There was an even longer silence. 'Oh well sir, that's different. We'll see what can be done.' He sent me downstairs with his secretary who organised the hat at cost while the floor manager fell apart in a fury.

Drag, radical drag. In the early seventies, we celebrated the trannies of Stonewall. We all got into dresses. Good ones were so cheap then: Balenciaga or Dior for less than a fiver. As Mrs. Hippy, a southern belle, I didn't get very far, but the dress gave me confidence and two years later I won the Alternative Miss World. Meanwhile in the studio, my friend Pat flung on dresses with abandon. Elegant drag with Doc. Martens could overturn a London bus. At a Canonbury dinner party, a bishop leaned over conspiratorially and said, 'What a nice dress'.

EVERYTHING YOU ALWAYS WANTED TO KNOW ABOUT SEX

The sex manual, like the coffee table book and the colour supplement, was fearfully straight. Doctor David R. Reuben's 1971 book was a great one:

> *The usual homosexual experience is mutual masturbation. It is fast, easy and requires a minimum amount of equipment. The chaps simply undress, get into bed and manipulate each other's penises to the point of orgasm. Three to five minutes should be enough for the entire operation.*

> *Few homosexuals use their real names, they generally go by aliases choosing first names with a sexual connotation; Harry, Dick, Peter are the most favoured. One drops to his knees, the other unzips his pants and a few moments later it's all over. No names, no faces, no emotions. A masturbation machine might do it better.*
> *Most homosexuals find their man-to-man sex unfulfilling, so they masturbate a lot. Much of their masturbation centres around the anus. The question, of course, is what to use for a penis. The answer is often found in the pantry. Carrots and cucumbers are pressed into ser-*

vice, forced into the anus lubricated with vegetable oil. Sausages, especially the milder varieties, are popular.

Some of the more routine items which find their way into the gastrointestinal systems of homosexuals via the exit are pens, pencils, lipsticks, pop bottles, ladies' electric shavers and enough other items to stock a small department store.

GAY ABANDON

Fucking became a full time leisure activity. Men discovered their sexuality. The Dionysian orgy was unleashed in the park, sauna and backroom. Johnny threw himself like a dancer into the bodies, naked except for his leather jacket with its silver studs. He was just twenty-one. That night he celebrated his coming of age. That night he would refuse no-one. One after another the men fucked him, and he loved it.

DRUGS

My upbringing was teetotal, there was a glass of wine at Christmas and that was it; my family never went to pubs. I was aware of drugs the moment I arrived in London in 1960. I'd read about them in Huxley's *Doors of Perception* in which he records his experiences on Peyote. When I moved up to Whitely Court near Russell Square, friends were making experiments with Morning Glory seeds and attempting to grow the Peyote cactus in Hampstead bathrooms. The adventurous went to West Indian clubs - if they could get in - as there was ganja there. They came back with exciting tales. I never went.

In 1964 hitch-hiking in California, I was picked up by a boy on a motorcycle who rolled joints. He gave me a packet of grass. I remember coming back to San Francisco not knowing how to smoke it - I rolled the most enormous joints of pure grass and got completely smashed.

I walked around the streets expecting to hallucinate but sadly it wasn't as dramatic as I'd hoped.

Drugs were everywhere. My mother had bottles of Mandrax. She used to off-load them saying: 'You're not sleeping properly, Derek. You must take some Mandrax.' The Mandrax used to disappear - my friends stole them; I was using them to go to sleep; they were using them for fucking!

Drugs in the clubs took off in the seventies. The bars were often used by dealers to push drugs. It was an easy sell.

Drugs and liberation were connected; *Oz* magazine for instance, brought together politics, drugs and sex. It was not possible to avoid them. Now I find myself neutral towards them; I don't think they damaged me and I can't believe they 'liberated' me - except for the moment.

I had to distance myself from Heterosoc and this was another weapon. Back in the sixties when there was no alcohol in the bars, drugs had a social value. The acid had a bad effect on a few people; some seemed to suffer from paranoia and an inability to grasp the world around them.

Of course, with treatment for HIV I'm ingesting enough drugs, and everything is laced with additives.

Is alcohol the best drug for controlling us? Certainly our lives revolved around the bars. The bars are so profitable; there is money to be made hand over fist. If there is a hierarchy of damage, grass came well below alcohol and tobacco.

Funny things can happen. My friend Karl came through customs at Gatwick loaded. He was asked to step through the metal detector gate and all the alarms went off; they couldn't understand why because he was carrying no metal objects. They pulled him in. Pornography was discovered in his suitcase and they found some acid.

The customs officer said, 'What are you doing here?' Karl said, 'I'm here on holiday'. They asked him to strip off and found he was wearing a cock-ring which had set the alarm off. The customs officer had his hands everywhere. He took his name and address and sent him on his way.

The next day he was rung up, everything was sent back to him - including the acid. The officer said 'Have a good holiday'.

Every now and again people fail to fulfil their statutory duty if they encounter an attractive young man.

SOMBRERO 1972

'Amadeo, more champagne': Vicki de Lambray, sitting in his vantage point, waves his hand at the patron of the Sombrero, almost the first licensed gay bar in London. Vicki was a plastic Buddha, ashen-pale with long lank hair and a high-pitched voice, his only conversation Ossie, David and Francis Bacon - particularly Francis who none of us met and who lurked in his leathers at the door of a party waiting to make a getaway to Soho. Vicki, who dropped names through a decade, was rumoured to be the lover of a Labour Peer (he arrived in the Peer's Rolls); was reputed to be a rent boy; was known to have spent time as a guest of Her Majesty in Parkhurst; and rang the newspapers the night he died to tell them he'd been murdered - no-one listened and he was found the next day dead from an generous overdose of mixed narcotics.

Vicki was the household god of the Sombrero. He would sit overlooking the glass dancefloor which was illuminated from beneath by coloured lights, waving at Ossie, Bianca, David, as they sang along to the song, 'I'm so vain, I think this song's all about me'.

Bianca, dressed like a matador waving a silver cane in the face of a bemused taxi driver at the door, and Amadeo - known universally as Armadillo - bead-eyed at the bottom of the steep staircase raking in the £££s - cash that HM Tax Inspectors would never see. José and Mañuel balancing the drinks on trays high above our heads like ballet dancers, Charles Chaplins of our Modern Time.

More champagne for Vicki, more champagne. 'Derek, do join us'. Vicki's falsetto. Francis, Ossie, David, all somewhere else, except in the conversation, the bottles of champagne piled up - a mountain of drink.

Meanwhile, all the boys on acid spinning round in their flared jeans barely caught sight of him out of the corners of their eyes.

The Sombrero was the first club that the respectably bisexual pop stars of the early seventies might bring their wives and boyfriends. Before that time they had been seen in a backroom in some other city. The Sombrero was glamorous enough to mention in an article in the *New Musical Express*.

And after the night ended you could hang out in Holland Walk - there was a strategically missing railing into the park - up and down just one last time; the police lurked, popping their heads over the school wall.

AMERICA 1974

The longest period I spent in Manhattan was the four months of Summer 1974. I walked around Manhattan exploring bookshops and galleries during the day and went out on the town every night. By the end of the summer I was living at night on the verge of being trapped in a dream of liberated sex, on the piers or at the Continental Baths, out at Fire Island, sleeping rough and meeting people on the beach. This nightlife was charged with an excitement far stronger than drugs.

As I stepped into the dark I entered the world of strangers. On the derelict piers I left the daylight world behind. The ground was strewn with glittering glass from the smashed windows. Every shadow was a potential danger; I kept my money in my shoe; walked through a succession of huge empty rooms, with young men often naked in the shafts of light which fell through the windows. The piers had their own beauty; surrounded by water they were a secret island.

Out at Fire Island the atmosphere was the same. The shrubs in the woods that lay along the shore were heavily scented, full of fireflies, silent floating will-o'-the-wisps. The silence and deep satisfaction of being alone attracted me as much as the possibility of a chance encounter.

I would spend every night wandering, then sit by the seashore watching the rising sun.

This world had a simplicity that I never encountered in 'civilised' surroundings. Living this way preserved a cherished silence. As the decade wore on, I grew further and further away from the social events, the cocktail parties and openings and even my own studio. Out alone at night, I was a traveller. Power, privilege, even good looks, and certainly money, disappeared in that dark.

The lid was off; the dance was on.

I had a friend who lived on Christopher Street in New York, two storeys up, opposite a public phone. The street was the cruisiest place and Ben would sit on a hot summer's afternoon and watch the boys walk by. If he saw one he fancied he'd ring the phone. More often than not the boy would stop, hesitate, then pick up the receiver. Ben would compliment him on his looks and engage in telephone sex. The boy would look around to see if he could find the author of the compliments. Ben succeeded in getting these lads to pull out their cocks, more often than not with a hard-on, and jerk off.

The Continental Baths was the most exciting club of the lot and host to the social register on Fridays. The Baths were on the West side above Columbus Circle, in an old building: eleven dollars entry. The dance floor was alongside a very large swimming pool with fountains, surrounded by beach chairs. Off to the side was a labyrinthine white-tiled Turkish bath whose corridors ended in pitch black; the scalding steam took your breath away. In the darkest recesses a continuous orgy was under way, but the heat was so searing only the most intrepid could get it up.

Besides the Turkish bath, there were saunas, a hundred bedrooms, a restaurant, a bar, a games room, and a hairdresser's, back-rooms with bunks, pitch-black orgy rooms and a sun-roof; on a weekend it would be packed.

It was possible to live there - and at eleven dollars a night cheaper than an hotel or apartment. I met one young man who had lived there for three months; he had only left the building a couple of times. Like the desert, though, the Baths played disturbing tricks; down there time dissolved you in the shadows. An afternoon passed in seconds.

The handsome drug dealers, sprawled out on their bunks gently masturbating, their doors slightly ajar to trap the unwary and, if you swallowed their bait, inhibitions cast aside, you'd be making love in that swimming pool packed with naked bodies.

Later in an apartment crawling with cockroaches, staring at the drained features of some Adonis whose smile had cracked like mud at the bottom of a dried-up lake, none of the fountains could restore the dream. This life could become as wearying as the treadmill in a rodent's cage; round and round we went in the land of Cockaigne.

In the Autumn, I left all this behind and came back to London.

SEBASTIAN

Most of our biography is located in fiction. Genet's prisoners, Cocteau's sailors; it was not possible to write in the first person, so we have a lack of information.

Historical biography is often in the hands of the unsympathetic, for instance Ellmann's Wilde. It is still quite common to read that the uncovering of a Queer life has diminished it. Beware of the executors of the estate.

I had criticism of this sort for my *Caravaggio*, and it haunts the criticism of Edward II's friendship with Gaveston - that could never be love. The sexuality of so many men was not loved in the history books.

No-one could be Queer and celebrated; Michelangelo, Leonardo, Shakespeare were all neutered. Hollywood invented heterosexual affairs for Michelangelo in *The Agony and the Ecstasy* and took forty years to reinstate Queer Caesar in *Spartacus*. This is why Hollywood is contemptible. Its ecstasy was exclusively heterosexual and reviewers connived - no-one spoke up, the words were taboo - for it not to be mentioned in the papers, the theatre, or television. Look at Rock Hudson's fate on their scrap-heap.

In 1976, the 'out' straight (God help us) film-maker Derek Jarman made one of the first heterosexual films ten years after heterosexual acts were finally decriminalised in private. Everyone was relieved that Heterosexuality could be talked about in the open. 15% of clergy are known to be straight and after two thousand years the church is coming to accept this. A member of the clergy can even live with a member of the opposite sex but musn't fuck. Things have got a little better for heterosexuals; there are several clubs run by gangsters where they can meet, they have one small newspaper - Straight News. It's even rumoured that one of the Royal Queers is straight.

Autumn 1976, my film *Sebastian* opened in Notting Hill to a rave review in *Gay News*:

Very occasionally there appears a film of such power and authority that one emerges from the cinema feeling somewhat shaken and disorientated... It is a very special, and indeed, a quite remarkable film that represents a milestone in the history of gay cinema.

The review was too kind but then nothing like this had been seen. At this time no-one had a video recorder, few people went to porn cinemas - in fact, there was only one in Soho (ironically called 'The Spartacus') where the young doormen would close the box office to fuck customers in the projection booth. Television was heavily censored, though one of the concessions made was to screen *The Naked Civil Servant*.

Sebastian didn't present homosexuality as a problem and this was what made it different from all the British films that had preceded it. It was also homoerotic. The film was historically important; no feature film had ventured here. There had been underground films, *Un Chant d'Amour* and *Fireworks*, but *Sebastian* was in a public space.

Although it is flawed and lacks any of the finesse of professional filmmaking, it altered peoples lives. It was to be ten years before it was shown on television. I was the last feature film-maker of my generation to have work shown by Channel 4. *Sebastian* was screened with the word 'mother-fucker' changed to 'mother's-boy', late at night with a warning, and without the erection.

Sebastian, the doolally Christian who refused a good fuck, gets the arrows he deserved. Can one feel sorry for this Latin closet case? Stigmata Seb who sports his wounds on a thousand altars like a debutante. All fags liked a good Sebastian. Mishima tried him on like leather chaps. Alberto Moravia said, 'this is a film Pier Paolo [Pasolini] would have loved to have made'.

The filming in Sardinia - £30,000 in briefcases from a shipping magnate - was hard, long and hot. The pivot of the film was Ken's hard-on; no-one had done this in a feature. Ken found his screen lover did not turn him on, so Gerald said 'I'll give it a blow' - they went behind a rock and Ken came back erect and glistening in the sunlight. The crew left saying I was making a porno film screaming 'fucking exploitation'.

I sat by my fire till the Sardinian shepherds drove their goats along the beach in the middle of the night. There were three hundred goats and they all had bells which rang in the starlit night. These were not church bells; they sounded like running water, the music of the spheres. Piero, the youngest of the shepherds, threw blankets over me and took me up to the top of the old Etruscan tower that commanded the sea to the west. There he held me and kissed me. By the time we returned to Rome, all the Sardinian shepherds had English lovers.

Ken's cock appeared at the bottom of the frame and projected at 1:1.85 was not seen by the censor. The love scene was ecstatic. A generation went to see these nine minutes of a regular guy in a regular cinema - except in the States, where love was rated 'S' for sex and the film was buried in porno houses where it pleased no-one.

Years later, a young man in Glasgow said that he had seen *Sebastian* on television; he had to turn the sound down because his parents were upstairs so he couldn't understand what was going on (despite the subtitles). He saw it later with the sound turned up but still didn't understand what the film was about; nevertheless he told me that it had changed his life.

TARNISHED SILVER

How compromised have you been in your film work?
I would have loved to have had real fucking in my films - I would have got off on it. Imagine all those teenagers jerking off in bed over their portable televisions.

There's a feeling in your films of 'how much can I get away with' like the opening scene in Edward II *where you have the two boys on the bed. Do you feel you've been able to make the films that you've wanted to make in the way you wanted to make them?*

I would have liked them to be more explicit, true films about our lives in the here and now. My demands were minimal. In *Angelic Conversation*, all I wanted to show was a screen kiss; I hadn't seen a romantic screen kiss between two men. In *Edward II*, I was held back by my reticence with the straight actors as much as the funding bodies - although they were worried about showing as much as I did.

Haven't you been trapped by the system; you made Edward II *for a pittance - £800,000. You're living the life of an exile from the film industry and yet you're still having to make your films to their requirements.*

Well, I *am* making them. Of the 'faggot' directors of my generation no-one made more. The compensation for making *Sebastian* for £30,000 or *Edward II* for £800,000 is that I can be certain that these films, which are involved in a struggle, will be shown thirty or forty years from now.

The criticism might be that I was too negative. Fair enough, I understand that, but life isn't a bowl of cherries. I think that the films reflect the problems of living now. That's why I think *Salò* is so important; Pasolini shows his disaster. That's the bravest thing to do, isn't it? In the end you can't help people with chit chat.

My *Salò* is not in film; it might be this book. It was easier for Pasolini to get the resources because the Italians were interested in the minds of their film-makers. No-one's interested in the minds of film-makers here. They never were.

Why do you think that is?

Our film involved itself in ideas, but these were never taken seriously in the shadow of Hollywood. A shared language was the problem. Hollywood is not seen as foreign film-making and is wedded to product and entertainment.

The battle is about imaging a generation - what is taken from the past and how it is projected, what is promoted and what isn't. In order to make Queer films and be a Queer artist Heterosoc drove me into a corner. Heterosoc could transgress and be applauded for it. There is more violation in any Hollywood film than mine.

Are you or your films martyred? Because your interventions are personalised, how effective are you?
Not very effective - because the world is increasingly run for profit. The worst advertise their integrity and others believe them.

So why do you continue?
Because when all is said and done, this is what will be remembered. I could have been much more effective in the short term if I had joined them, I can see that. On the other hand I would have made no serious intervention if I had.

What would joining them have done to you?
I would have made a short term gain. There is desperation in this. Desperation because of time running out, desperation for a generation, desperation for myself. You are talking to someone who is desperate, who is near to tears.

WITHOUT TWO PEAS TO RUB TOGETHER

Sebastian must have been the only feature film made without a telephone. Funds were short. Mid-decade found me homeless, living in a rooming house in Earls Court run by a lady who had taught the King of Egypt to dance. *Sebastian* opened with a riot at the Locarno film festival, the audience shouting and stamping their feet all through the screening. The best thing to come out of it was the founding of gay lib in Switzerland! Punk was upon us.

OPEN T-SHIRT TO DEREK JARMAN
FROM VIVIENNE WESTWOOD

JUBILEE - I had been to see it once and thought it the most boring and therefore disgusting film I had ever seen. I went to see it again for, after all, hadn't you pointed your nose in the right direction? Rather than deal with spectacular crap as other film-makers do, you had looked at something here and now of absolute relevance to anybody in England with a brain still left; let's call it soul. I first tried very hard to listen to every word spoken in the flashbacks to Eliz. I. What were you saying? Eliz: "This vision exceedeth by far all expectation. Such an abstract never before I spied" and so she went on - Fal de ray la lu lullay the day! And John Dee spoke "poetry" according to Time Out *(those old left-overs from a radio programme, involving a panel of precocious sixth formers, called* Cabbages and Kings, *whose maturity concerns being rather left from a position of safety) though even now I can remember no distinguishing phrase from amongst the drone, only the words "down, down, down" (Right on).*

And Aerial who flashed the sun in a mirror, and considered a diamond and had great contact lenses: "Consider the world's diversity and worship it. By denying its multiplicity, you deny your own true nature. Equality prevails not for God but for mans' sake" - consider that! What an insult to my VIRILITY! *I'm a punk, man (and you use the values you give to punks as a warning, I am supposed to see old Elizabeth's England as some state of grace? Well, I rather consider that all this grand stuff and looking at diamonds is something to do with a gay (which you are) boy's love of dressing up and playing at charades. (Does he have a cock between his legs or doesn't he? kinda thing).*

As to the parts about the near future there were 2 good lines in it. Adam (kid): "I don't care about the money I just don't wanna get ripped off" (funny) and Angel or Sphinx to Adam: "Don't sign up, etc... Life is more exciting on the streets." Excepted that no-one would want any dealings with the clichéd figment of your fantasies: Borgia Ginze, what did the streets have to offer? Well, they then pinched a car to go visit a nutter with a garden of plastic flowers. Then they went to the roof of a towerblock to give out the kind of simplistic spiel Alf Garnett, or rather Mick Jones of the Clash, gives out. Is that your comment about the street? What you read in the music press? Good - the low budget, independent, using friends, non-equity aspect. Good that the non-equity members weren't required to act but allowed to say their lines as if reading from a little book inside their head, because what happened by result of this acting, as against some acting ability was that the performances depended for strength on how much humanity the people behind the role possessed. Thus Jordan and Helen were good whereas Jenny Runacre's mediocrity of spirit blud-

geoned through.

Albeit - these aspects of your approach and style were anarchical. I am not interested in how interestingly you say nothing (the Rule Brittania *Eurovision Song Contest was good because you said something - nationalism is vile and Elizabeth II is a commercial con trick. Just like E1).*

An anarchist must say, "trust yourself" It's the place to start. But self-indulgence is not the answer. You have to be brave and you are only a little. You have to cut the crap and not the cheese and chuck out - UGH - for instance those Christian crucifixion fixations (sex is not frightening, honest) - "the pervasive reek of perverse and esoteric artiness, the delight in degradation and decay simply for its beauty when stylised. An irresponsible movie. Don't remember punk this way" (all quoted from Chris Brazier in Melody Maker*).*

But I ain't insecure enough nor enough of a voyeur to get off watching a gay boy jerk off through the titillation of his masochistic tremblings. You pointed your nose in the right direction then you wanked. It was even more boring than Uncle Tom Don Letts' even lower budget film.

2ND NOVEMBER 1975, THE DEATH OF PIER PAOLO PASOLINI

As I perceived him in the middle of that solitude, that oblivion, to which I was reduced, I screamed 'pity please' as in dreams when all dignity is lost.

The murder of Pier Paolo at Ostia - by a gang who's movements were covered up by the Italian judiciary - was a light extinguished in the room of our minds. The death of our poet, our historian, our film-maker, murdered by Heterosoc; Wilde, Marlowe, Caravaggio, Tchaikovsky and now Pasolini all murdered. Break the circle of death.

In the forensic photo, Pasolini, dishevelled sacrifice, run over by a boy in a car again and again and again to obliterate his identity.

Waiting last night for a cab at Hampstead ponds, 2:30am on a cold December night, there's shouting in the car park and a car drives past with six young men; joyriders? One winds the window down and shouts 'fuckin' puff' and throws a piece of concrete at me that crashes on the pavement and bounces into the bushes. The car roars into the night, It's silent again.

GAY RIOT SHAKES THE CITY; GAY NEWS, 31ST MAY 1979

San Francisco: A troubled calm has returned to San Francisco after a gay protest march led to the worst city rioting America has seen for ten years.

Around 4000 homosexuals attacked the City Hall smashing its windows with iron bars and parking meters torn up from the streets, breaking into offices and destroying official records. Thirty police cars were wrecked or set on fire during the riot.

The City Council met urgently to lay plans for a curfew and consider declaring a state of emergency.

This outburst of violence followed a surprise jury decision earlier in the day at the end of the trial of Dan White, former policeman, city official and double killer. Last November, White, aged 33, shot dead two of his political opponents - gay city councillor Harvey Milk and Liberal Mayor George Moscone.

The jury found White not guilty of murder but only of "voluntary manslaughter". The sentence passed on him means that he is likely to be released within three years.

BLASPHEMY 1978

Gay News was first published priced ten new pence in 1972. Now we were able to explore our problems and celebrate our achievements without being contextualised by Heterosoc. Throughout the decade, our bookshops and papers were subject to police harassment. *Gay News* itself was to fall foul of Mary Whitehouse's Festival of Light in the prosecution for blasphemy of James Kirkup's poem *The Love that Dares to Speak its Name.*

For the last time
I laid my lips around the tip
of that great cock, the instrument
of our salvation, our eternal joy

As long as our sexuality was contained, we could be exploited; the authorities never forgot to let you know that. A bookshop or a poem could bring down the whole silly weight of authority. Heterosoc was under assault.

Jane Ellison reported for the *Evening Standard:*

Members of the gay picket who have been demonstrating outside the Old Bailey, where Denis Lemon was given a nine month suspended sentence today, say he has been found guilty because he is gay. Lemon, 32, editor of the homosexual paper Gay News, *was found guilty of blasphemous libel, but his supporters insist that gay people everywhere have been on trial this week.*

He was found guilty by ten votes to two. "It was what we expected," he said leaving the court. "Two votes on our side was a minor victory," he smiled pinning a badge onto his lapel. It bore the words: GAY NEWS FIGHTS ON, framing the face of Mary Whitehouse.

On the way out they passed, like warriors, within six feet of each other. "I am rejoicing" said Mary Whitehouse, her eyes glinting behind her spectacles.

"I feel slightly shattered and empty", said Lemon, his face white with strain. "I'm not sure what to do. It is not the evening to sit alone at home and listen to Bruckner is it?"

WAS THERE ANY TIME FOR LOVE IN THE SEVENTIES?

In 1979, after my warehouse burnt to the ground, I moved to Soho. I had made three small films alongside the system, full of flaws and good intentions. I had built my life away from Heterosoc, fighting the limitations of the feature film. Perhaps we could build, dare to build a life of our own.

There were gay communes. In Railton Road, Brixton - the whole street had been squatted. Now we had, or were about to have, lesbian and gay film festivals, gay olympics and academic chairs.

I cut my hair short, took off my earrings, put on a leather jacket and, armed with KY and poppers, took off into the night. The decade had been good to us in spite of the setbacks; the blasphemy trial of *Gay News*, the murders of Pasolini and Harvey Milk.

I was happy.

1980s

HIV+

By the early eighties two men having sex was no longer perceived as a transgression. HIV changed that.

I wouldn't wish the eighties on anyone, it was the time when all that was rotten bubbled to the surface. If you were not at the receiving end of this mayhem, you could be unaware of it. It was possible to live through the decade preoccupied by the mortgage and the pence you saved on your income tax.

It was also possible for those of us who saw what was happening to turn our eyes in a different direction; but what, in another decade, had been a trip to the clap clinic was now a trip to the mortuary.

Ten years into the epidemic, HIV has killed more young men in the States than the Vietnam war. At the moment - New Year 1992 - there have been a quarter of a million admitted deaths - many more are unrecognised, or deliberately misattributed.

AIDS showed up an inheritance for a confusion. Faced with the prospect of writing about it, I faltered; there were too many stories I wanted to record. There had been no disease since syphilis so trapped in preconception and sexual stigma; exaggerated by the (erroneous) perception that it was only transmitted between homosexual men - 'AIDS, AIDS, AIDS,' shouted the kids in the playground, 'Arse Injected Death Syndrome'. In the first few years of this epidemic, your neighbours were cast out of the city. I've kept these sketches simple as the full weight of it would drown you.

I tested HIV+ on 22 December 1986. I became frightened of myself, I was potentially lethal and all the advice I got was a muddle. I was told not to test, then I was told to keep the test results secret. That first day I made my status public, I walked into a crowded room and held my breath - I knew that if I embraced these friends of mine they were not at risk, but did they? Should I hold their children and risk terrifying them?

All life became a problem, and I solved this by shutting my physical self like a clam. For a while I could have been a model for the Conservative Family Association.

I watched life going by, people falling in love and I was no longer part of it. I was living in another land, no-man's land. These were hard years.

I allowed myself to be hemmed in; my mouth was open, I was talking, but my body was in prison. Sometimes I went to a bar, but in the bar, in the smoke and noise, all anyone talked about was film and film and then, now and again, some shaking youth would tell me secretly that he was HIV+. We would talk practically - I was always practical - and then the noise became too loud and, with blessed relief, I went up to the Heath and sat on a tree and watched the moon and the jets crossing and re-crossing the clouds. It was here that calm prevailed in all the insanity of the ABC of HIV.

One of the ironies of the HIV epidemic was that sex was now being talked about - but not honestly. We were still at a disadvantage in the media.

When Philip Core died, Dr. Jonathan Miller made the remark on a television obituary that his openly homosexual painting was 'a matter of taste' but, 'he felt a revulsion for homosexuality as a jew would feel a revulsion for pork'.

A RESPONSIBLE TABLOID

One of the many confusions in the perception of the epidemic was that in the public mind it coincided with the visibility of sex and sexual libera-tion. It was this visibility that enabled us to deal with the epidemic. If it had occurred in the last century, it would have been as catastrophic and much harder to fight because of sexual oppression. In 1979, it was impos-sible to know you might be infecting yourself with an unknown virus in The Subway - the wildest of the clubs. The virus wasn't to be isolated until 1984 by which time friends were dying.

Censure informs the commentary on HIV. When we first learnt that something was going wrong, it was far away in America. Known as GRID - Gay Related Immune Deficiency - the name was the beginning of mis-information which fed into the media so that HIV has always been iden-tified with gay men. Even recently, the *Daily Mail* said that HIV had no connection with heterosexual sex, ignoring what is happening in Africa, or Great Britain for that matter where a quarter of all new diagnoses are heterosexual. The *Mail* is quite happy to put its readers at risk.

And what was happening in this country in the early eighties?

There was a confusion in which we acted responsibly. All our energy was spent looking after friends and raising money. It was *we* who provided *you* with the information that may have saved *your* life.

Perhaps the first reference in the British Press to the new illness appeared on 28th May 1982 in *Capital Gay*, a weekly free-sheet, distributed in the bars and clubs of London. These quotations are from that paper, the headings are mine.

A MYSTERIOUS NEW DISEASE
28th May 1982

The latest medical research into the killer disease known as Gay Cancer suggests links with sleeping around and the use of amyl nitrite poppers... So far the only case reported in this country was traced back to the United States... Public health officials are also discovering a "laundry list" of other strange diseases that are striking gay men, apparently associated with a dysfunction of the patients' immune systems... But the mystery surrounding the newly-discovered cancer and other diseases remains.

HAVE YOU EVER THOUGHT OF BECOMING A STATISTIC?
30th July 1982

Latest reports from the United States say 37 heterosexuals have been diagnosed as suffering from the gay cancer and related diseases.

HEALTH CARE WITH A SONG AND A DANCE
26th November 1982

A massive entertainment machine is being launched to raise cash for research into Immune Deficiency and Kaposi's Sarcoma.
The target is to raise £100,000 to sponsor research into the mystery ill-

nesses that have killed four gay Londoners in the last year...The new charity, called the Terry Higgins Trust, is named after the first Londoner to die from Immune Deficiency... Immune Deficiency made him succumb to a parasitic pneumonia - the same illness that recently killed disco star Patrick Cowley, as we reported last week.

BLOODSCARE

27th May 1983

The directors of Britain's blood transfusion centres have issued a request asking gay men who have multiple sexual partners not to give blood. They are also asking heterosexuals with multiple sexual partners, and people from Haiti not to give blood.

THE WOMAN WHO DIDN'T FIT

27th January 1984

Two new cases of AIDS have been confirmed in Britain, both in patients who died last month. This brings the total number of cases in this country to 33, including 18 deaths.

One of the new cases was a 44-year-old gay man who died from Kaposi's Sarcoma in London. The other was a 40-year-old woman who doesn't fit into any of the main risk categories.

U.S. TEAM FINDS VIRUS

27th April 1984

American scientists believe they have found the cause of AIDS which could lead to a vaccine and a cure for the disease which has killed nearly 2,000 Americans and 22 people in Britain.

CONDOMS

28th September 1984

Condoms have many uses. You can inflate them as balloons for indiscrete dinner-parties or write apt slogans on them in deep purple eyeliner. But if they are to be more than decorative you need to take some trouble to learn how to use them correctly. The main problem, as I see it, is that those gay men who stand to gain most from a shield against semen have to persuade their partners to take that trouble and, in particular, partners they haven't met before.

THE BETRAYAL OF THE STRAIGHT PRESS
23rd November 1984

In the last week the straight media has devoted more column centimetres and more airtime to the subject of AIDS than it has for a very long time. And yet throughout the time we have been suffering from the disease they seem to have learnt little.

Worst, as usual, was The Sun *which still calls it "the gay plague", although listeners to BBC World Service could have heard their science correspondent correct that mistake.*

But there seemed to be no national newspaper or broadcasting organisation, except the World Service, which reported the facts calmly, honestly and accurately. Even the BBC's Radio Four left listeners with the impression that 'wicked' homosexuals were killing 'innocent' straights. There was little indication that innocent homosexuals were suffering, and dying, because of AIDS.

They were apparently oblivious to the physical and psychological pain which the disease is causing among gay people, and their sloppy reporting simply made the situation worse.

They ignored how seriously gay people are taking the disease, and the practical steps being taken by organisations and individuals to control the spread of the disease and to help AIDS patients and their loved ones.

SAFE SEX GUIDELINES
14th December 1984

1. Have sex with fewer men.

2. Avoid anal sex, except possibly with your regular partner.

3. Have sex only with men whom you know to be in good health and who have had few other sexual partners.

4. Avoid sex with men who have been sexually active in North America in the last three years.

5. Since the virus has been found even in saliva, perhaps the only safe sex is mutual masturbation, body rubbing and dry kissing.

A PSYCHOLOGICAL MILESTONE
14th December 1984

The total number of AIDS cases in Britain has gone over the psychological milestone of 100 cases.

The Department of Health told us this week that the total number is now 102, of whom 44 are dead.

The number of cases is following the American pattern almost identically with a doubling of figures every six months. That means we have to plan for 400 cases within a year.

TELECOMICS
15th March 1985

Gay Switchboard was left limping along on just one phone line last Thursday and Friday after telephone engineers refused to repair their other four lines - for fear of catching AIDS!

MAN KILLED AFTER AIDS TAUNT
2nd August 1985

An 18-year-old Coventry man, who thought he had caught AIDS after drinking from the same bottle as a gay man, punched and killed him, Warwick Crown Court heard on Friday.

Neil McDougall pleaded guilty to the manslaughter of Peter Davis and was sentenced to three months in a detention centre. It is unusual in cases of manslaughter for the killer to be given less than a five year prison sentence.

TO TEST OR NOT TO TEST
2nd August 1985

The Government is about to make widely and freely available a test for the antibody to the AIDS-related virus - which poses the British gay community one of the toughest dilemmas yet caused by AIDS.

Opinion is divided on whether or not apparently healthy gay men should take the test in the interests of public health, or whether they should avoid the test to protect themselves, their homes and their jobs as well as the balance of their minds.

THE FOOLS AMONGST US
16th August 1985

The Hippodrome club in Leicester Square, which for 18 months has held a gay night every Monday, has sacked a man for being HTLV-3 positive.

"I realise that 80% of the people who come here on a Monday have probably got it," said Roger Howe, managing director and Peter Stringfellow's right-hand man, "but I didn't want to employ someone who could pass on the disease. We get thousands of people in here."

GOVERNMENT MINISTER DIES OF AIDS
30th August 1985

Former Government Minister Lord Avon died of AIDS last Saturday at St. Stephen's Hospital in Fulham.

The 54-year-old son of former Prime Minister Anthony Eden was forced to leave politics earlier this year when failing health meant he could no longer carry out his duties in the House of Lords.

He was the Tory Minister in the Lords responsible for steering the Local Authority Bill for scrapping the GLC through the House, a job now being done by Lord Elton.

CLOSE THE GAY BARS
29th November 1985

A secret group of Tory MPs are putting pressure on the government to bring in new laws that will close all of the country's gay pubs and clubs.

The campaign led by Geoffrey Dickens, the outspoken MP for Littleborough and Saddleworth, has been revealed by the national press even though the members of the group only wanted to work behind the scenes rather than in the glare of publicity.

CONCENTRATION CAMPS
20th December 1985

The case of a man with AIDS, now being held in a remote isolation hospital against his will and without a hearing, renewed alarm over

Government powers taken last March.

Powers to detain people with AIDS (PWAs) in hospital, more drastic than powers taken anywhere else in the world, were sharply attacked by the country's top medical and counselling experts when they were first published.

The first use of those powers in a Manchester magistrates court last Saturday fully justified those early fears.

The man was admitted to Monsall isolation hospital, North Manchester three weeks ago. Last week he told hospital staff that he wanted to leave the gloomy and remote Victorian hospital and move back home.

But a senior consultant moved swiftly to prevent him. Using the new Public Health (Infectious Diseases) Regulations 1985, he applied to Manchester's medical officer for health. She sought the approval of the Chair of the City Council's Environmental Health Services Committee - a formality - and then went to court.

In an unusual Saturday morning hearing, magistrate Thomas Jones granted the order detaining the man for three weeks.

UNDER THE SIGN OF THE PINK TRIANGLE

The slow-witted approach to the HIV epidemic was the result of a thousand years of Christian malpractice and the childlike approach of the church to sexuality. If any single man was responsible, it was Augustine of Hippo who murdered his way to a sainthood spouting on about the sins located in his genitals.

Those who thought otherwise, that sexuality was to be celebrated, were executed or pushed into the shadows. The battle goes on with Augustine's pack hunting in the debased tabloids. Augustine was joined by other demented saints.

The passions in fact are dishonourable since the soul is more damaged and degraded by sins than the body is by illness... Real pleasure is only in accordance with nature. When God has abandoned someone every-thing is inverted, for I tell you that such people are even worse than murderers. The murderer only separates soul from body but these peo-ple destroy the soul within the body. Whatever sin you mention you will not name one the equal of this and if those who suffer it really perceive what was being done to them, they would rather die a thousand deaths.

— SAINT JOHN CHRYSOSTOM

It is important that this history is not left in the hands of theologians who can hide these ugly-minded men behind walls of Latin and Greek. Their legacy allowed us to be sent to the gas chambers without a murmur. The Allies after they 'liberated' the concentration camps put us back in civil prisons to serve our sentences for our Queer 'crimes'. The concentration camps were invented in the minds of the inquisition and will never be understood unless they are seen as the centre of a Christian tradition. Those of us who are HIV+ are in another kind of concentration camp.

5TH NOVEMBER 1991

Last night it was very cold, fireworks and rockets flaring in the sky. I went up to the Heath early because I was fed up getting in so late, I would be back before midnight which makes it easier to get up in the morning.

Two men had built a bonfire, others were standing round keeping warm. A young man stopped me. He very much liked *Edward II*. I thanked him and he introduced me to his friend.

'What are you doing up here?'

'Oh, I'm being shown the sights. I moved to London two months ago and my friend's showing me the sights.'

He seemed happy to meet me. We talked about film and then he told me his story.

'I'm a miner's son. It's been difficult coming down from the north to London.'

'Well, I know a bit about that. People are less friendly down here, aren't they?'

'Yes, that's certain.'

'What was life like up there?'

He laughed: 'I fucked all the boys in my school, every single one of them. They are all married now except for me - my father joined in! Isn't life strange?'

We talked for half an hour and then he said, 'I want to tell you a terrible story... I've got a boyfriend back home.'

'Yes, everyone up here has got a boyfriend. Who doesn't have a boyfriend?' I joked.

'Three years ago he was diagnosed HIV+. His doctor, who knew he was gay, organised a test for him. When he went back two weeks later for the results, he was told he had the virus. The doctor was a born-again Christian and he said my friend should give up his homosexuality and become a Christian. He didn't do that and we coped for three years. A month ago he was called up and asked to go and have further tests by the hospital. He was tested and then re-tested and called back to be told he had never had the virus. They had been investigating the doctor, who had been giving young men who he knew were gay false positive results.'

THE POLICE CONSTABLE'S CESSPIT

Only in Britain could a provincial policeman make crass moral pronouncements, be applauded for it by the press and government, and end up knighted.

Whilst straight liberals knocked back the affluence and slept through Thatcher's Terror, mortgaged to a false vision of the past, we Queers found ourselves on the frontline once again. How many killed themselves? How many were beaten to death? Assaulted? Thrown out of their homes and jobs? Imagine finding yourself refused access to your dying lover by a family that disowned him years ago and then being thrown out of your home by them because it was in his name.

'What did you do in the war, daddy?'
'I proved my manhood by bashing the homos.'

Here are some of the headlines from the front pages of the *Sun*, the *News of the World*, the *People*, *Daily Mail*, *Daily Mirror*, the *Star* and *Daily Express*. In italics another voice, the gay press.

AIDS BLOOD IN M&S PIES PLOT

THE NIGHT I MET MP IN GAY CLUB

SEX BOYS FOR SALE AT QUEEN'S GROCERS

GAY SANTA GETS SACK

18 VICE BOYS IN AIDS REVENGE

PULPIT POOFS CAN STAY

VILE BOOK IN SCHOOL -
PUPILS SEE PICTURES OF GAY LOVERS

EASTENDER PAT'S GAY SECRET

The BBC has withdrawn a play showing a positive gay relationship between two teenagers, which had been intended for broadcast on schools' television.

6 PALACE SERVANTS IN AIDS DANGER

James Anderton said on BBC Radio 4's Sunday programme that 'divine inspiration' told him to say, in a speech on AIDS, that people are 'swirling around in a cesspit of their own making'.

EDWARD GIRL'S DAD IS GAY

More than 20 police raided the Royal Vauxhall Tavern in south London on Friday night wearing masks and rubber gloves.

SWIM POOL GUARD IN AIDS HORROR

The Prime Minister Margaret Thatcher has told the House of Commons that 'morals' do matter in AIDS and people can, by their own conduct, avoid catching the disease.

AIDS MENACE: HE CARRIES KILLER VIRUS
YET WORKS WITH SICK KIDS

Hardline Tories are making new moves to sack MP Harvey Proctor following his arrest over allegations that he hired rent boys for spanking sessions.

POLL VERDICT ON GAY VICARS: KICK 'EM OUT

The victim went with his attacker to the Rose Garden in the park and it was there that he was stabbed through the neck with a broken bottle. His killer then savagely beat John about the face using the bottle to try and make his face unrecognisable.

HOLIDAY ISLE IN AIDS TERROR

People with AIDS are finding it so difficult to get hold of the drug AZT that thieves have tried to steal it from a London hospital.

AIDS: GOOD SAMARITAN VICTIM

Gay men have been sent home from hospitals without treatment because some doctors and surgeons are scared of catching AIDS.

CHARLES' VALET DIES OF AIDS

Two gay men who got 'married' on TV last weekend have provoked the wrath of the raving right who denounced the ceremony as an 'outrage' and 'utterly irresponsible'. Mary Whitehouse claimed that 'In the light of AIDS and the need to bolster the traditional family relationship, this kind of thing is utterly irresponsible'.

GAYS IN FEAR: THEY DREAD REVENGE AFTER ATTACK ON BOY

Education Secretary Kenneth Baker said that the book Jenny Lives With Eric and Martin *is "blatant homosexual propaganda..."*

MANIAC RAMBO RYAN WAS MY GAY LOVER

Bullets fired from a revolver bounced off the walls of the London Apprentice pub in East London in a dramatic attack at the weekend.

MY GAY LOVE FOR BRUISER TYSON

The Prime Minister Margaret Thatcher mocked the 'right' to be gay during her main speech to the Conservative Party conference in Blackpool last week... 'Children who need to be taught to respect traditional moral values are being taught that they have an inalienable right to be gay.'

LESBIAN TEACHER HORROR

Twelve football hooligans launched a frenzied attack on people queueing for Britain's premier gay nightspot, Heaven, while gangs made two separate attacks on people near the Backstreet leather club in the East End.

IT'S EASTBENDERS: GAY MEN TO STIR UP TV SOAP

Two gay teenagers were fined for kissing in the street after a prosecution at Bow Street Court.

GAY LOVERS ON ROYAL YACHT

The first-ever opinion poll of its kind shows that the Tories and Labour are neck-and-neck in the popularity stakes with lesbians and gay men who are out and about in London.

DI'S DRESS MAN DIES IN AIDS CENTRE

Three thousand pounds worth of damage was caused to the house of veteran drag performer Terry Latour on Thursday when his house in south east London was fire-bombed.

SCANDAL OF GAY VICARS

The General Synod voted overwhelmingly for a 'compromise' motion which condemned gay sex but did not back moves to defrock gay clergy. The motion said that homosexual genital acts "fall short" of the Christian ideal that "sexual intercourse is an act of total commitment which belongs properly within a permanent married relationship".

GAY SENATOR SHAME

A man was kidnapped whilst cruising on Hampstead Heath and kept hostage for 14 hours by his attackers who punched and kicked him before forcing him to commit humiliating acts.

AIDS: BOY GEORGE IS TESTED FOR KILLER PLAGUE

Thirty people wearing rubber gloves - some policemen, some from Customs and Excise - raided a south London sauna last week, smashing up the rest room, arresting one employee and 10 customers - some of whom were photographed - and confiscating all membership cards.

SECRET OF NEWSBOY KILLER'S GAY PAL

Four men have been arrested after vicious attacks near King's Cross station on Sunday night in which one man was hospitalised after being stabbed in the neck.

MORE CHANNEL 4 SHOCKERS: THEY BUY TWO GAY FILMS FOR SHOWING UNCUT

Mary Whitehouse thought it 'deeply offensive' that the two films Sebastian and Jubilee were allowed to be shown. 'They were by far the worst films ever to be shown on TV,' said Mrs Whitehouse. 'For violence and sexual explicitness they were outrageous.'

VILEST OF THE VILE:
FOUR FIENDS KILL RENT BOY JASON IN AN ORGY

Customers and staff in West End gay pubs and clubs are facing a wave of police intimidation as they look for evidence for a murder case.

HARTY'S LOVER DEMANDS FORTUNE

The Sun *'newspaper' front page headline 'pulpit poofs can stay' is unlikely to encourage anti-gay hatred, the Press Council ruled last week.*

THE LAST DAYS OF ROCK HUDSON

Chief Rabbi Sir Immanuel Jakobovits has made an astonishing attack on gay people, people with AIDS and people who are HIV antibody positive. The spiritual leader of Britain's 330,000 Jews wants new laws against homosexuals, and he accuses HIV infected people of deliberately spreading the virus so as to find 'safety in numbers'.

GAY WOLFMAN GETS HIS CLAWS INTO HOLLY

A death threat was issued to the leader of an Ealing gay group after the News of the World *'newspaper' printed a lying story claiming that the group was making a council-funded 'raunchy gay video'.*

I'D SHOOT MY SON IF HE HAD AIDS, SAYS VICAR

'You can catch AIDS from lavatory seats and insect bites' was the wild claim of the Mail on Sunday's *front-page story, sparking off a furious response from gay activists and AIDS specialists.*

QUEEN'S COMIC IN RENT BOY SHAME

Doors were slammed and bolted, shutting frightened customers inside when a violent mob of thugs stormed the Royal Vauxhall Tavern pub on Saturday night.

KINKY VICAR'S GAY PLAYTIME

Old Bailey judge Michael Argyle branded the gay victim of a savage street attack as a 'little sodomite from Glasgow'.

EXCLUSIVE! LIBERACE AND PAL WHO DIED OF AIDS

A gay man was found murdered in Brixton on Sunday dressed in a green hospital gown. He was strangled but police will be unable to come up with the exact cause and time of death. Scandalous action by London pathologists who have refused to carry out a post-mortem on the dead man is frustrating police enquiries. They will not go near the body because they fear they may catch AIDS.

NORM'S CHAPLAIN PAL SEDUCED BOY PRIEST IN HIS JUMBO-SIZED BED

The flames of hatred in the Church of England's anti-gay witch-hunt were fanned afresh this week by the House of Laity. They congratulated those bishops who refuse to ordain homosexuals and called on the House of Bishops to make a similar statement.

LORDSHIP SPENDS £4,000 ON GAY NIGHT

Leading right-wing backbencher Nicholas Winterton MP has tabled a parliamentary motion attacking government health education on AIDS and saying 'the time is long overdue for the Government to condemn unnatural and unacceptable sexual practices'.

TOP LAWYER EXPOSED IN RENT BOY SCANDAL

A sinister campaign from far-right churchmen has succeeded in ousting the Lesbian and Gay Christian Movement from its premises. The Bishop of London's official representatives repeatedly referred to the movement as 'a bunch of poofs'.

RENT BOYS SHOCK

Anti-gay religious zealots are carrying out a leafleting campaign in Lambeth claiming that the council's 'policy drive to promote homosexuality is depriving the needy of food'.

AIDS STORM OVER A PONTIN'S LIFEGUARD

Customs officers contaminated nearly $1000 worth of AZT and

Acyclovir when they detained a gay American with AIDS at Heathrow Airport last week.

Nigel Lawson, the Chancellor of the Exchequer, defended the infamous Section 28... On the Walden Interview he said: 'There are groups of people who seek very aggressively to promote homosexuality, to proselytise in favour of homosexuality; even, in some cases, to brainwash children... Many parents find that deeply offensive and the question was whether children should be protected from that.'

JUDGE QUITS OVER HIS GAY AFFAIR

A pregnant Australian lesbian, who has been living in Britain with her English girlfriend for five years, faces deportation if the Home Office cannot be persuaded to reverse their cruel decision.

SODOM AND GOMORRAH

The Government is introducing the most serious legal attack on our rights since male homosexuality was outlawed more than 100 years ago... It gives succour to every bigot and tinpot dictator in the country who wants to go queerbashing.

STORM OVER EASTENDER RENT BOY FILTH:
GET THIS GARBAGE OFF TV

A Tory MP shouted out that the arson attack on Capital Gay was 'quite right' and when Labour MPs challenged Elaine Kellett-Bowman (Conservative, Lancaster) she explained: 'I am quite prepared to say and affirm that there should be an intolerance of evil.'

And so it went as you hid behind the *Independent* and the *Guardian*, like those good Germans who never heard the windows smashing in the crystal night.

A CONVERSATION WITH
DR. MATTHEW HELBERT, 1988.

November. The TV news carries film of a fire at King's Cross station, sudden, unnatural death overtakes the commuters. Why were they there? Why them? Is there a connection? Death out of the blue is horrendous to those outside but perhaps it is easier to die this way than with the uncertain threat of HIV.

I'm in the arena, the crowds are watching. My death is an entertaining statistic, something to cast a shadow before the second cup of tea at breakfast. It's quite impossible to communicate the feeling I have. I have not died so what can I tell you about death that you cannot imagine for yourself? HIV has brought it a little nearer in my mind, that's all. I'm more aware of my death as I shave in the mirror in the morning - in fact I've made a new mirror which has the Buddah sitting on top of it between two large pearls.

Thornton Wilder explores the 'random' connections of death in his book *The Bridge of San Luis Rey*. The bridge snapped and threw a dozen people to their deaths in the gorge below; why were they there at that moment in time? Perhaps something in their lives might tell us.

I join the statistics of those the virus has sought out.

The virus is an adventurer; it'll climb mountains and cross seas - it caught up with me, or at least I became aware of it, a year ago. It had already met up with close friends of mine; several died, amongst them the painter Mario Dubsky. None of us, apart from one or two very close friends, realised Mario was dying until it was over.

Mario had been extremely troubled in the years before. In a pub one evening he shouted at me that I had not spent enough time with him at his exhibition in Camberwell. I said I had thought he was busy and had better people to talk to than old friends. He said I'd betrayed him - we'd all betrayed him.

I don't know if he knew he was dying at that moment; he stormed out leaving the people in the pub wondering what he was going on about. That was the last I saw of him. There was no sign he was ill.

Other friends have just disappeared before anyone knew. One young man died of pneumonia - it seemed strange at the time as he was in his early twenties and very strong. In a way I hope that's what happens to me.

I worry about blindness and the degeneration of the mental faculties; I worry about the disfigurement of Kaposi's Sarcoma - one of my acquaintances had this when the virus was first isolated, and I'm ashamed to say I hardly dared look at him.

I'm not afraid of death but I am afraid of dying. Pain can be alleviated by morphine but the pain of social ostracism cannot be taken away.

Do you anticipate things being taken away from you, a diminishing?
My happy-go-lucky life has already been stolen by the virus.

My friend Malcolm Leigh told me of a Norwegian he knew who walked to the sea each day with a folding chair; he sat watching the horizon till sunset waiting for death.

I find isolation a consolation; the idea of the hospital and the socialisation of my death makes me unhappy; to have to meet all those new people and be subjected to the sort of jolly entertainment you describe terrifies me. I always hated pubs. I only went to them for the boys, nothing else. I have always been a recluse.

When we were making *Sebastian* Umberto Tirelli, the Italian costumier, read my hand at a dinner. He said: 'You are an alien Derek... You will die violently'. I thought of this often on the Heath. One night I was attacked by a gang. I stumbled to the station, covered in blood but I was still alive. I had avoided an acceptable end, in the tradition of Pasolini, the sacrificial victim. None of us ever imagined this violent virus.

Acquaintances met different ends: one set fire to himself, a sweet boy I took to Paris in the winter of '69; another was stabbed in the heart by a rent boy; one threw himself in front of the tube; some fell victim to drugs; none of us were struck by lightning. I slept quite often with Michele Lupo - the Italian who was given a life sentence for murdering several men last year. The rougher I was the more he enjoyed sex. I think he wanted to be annihilated in the orgasm.

I lived 'apart'. My studios brought me isolation, something I lost in the eighties. I've restored that again here by the sea; it's isolated but also accessible. I would hate this to be taken away.

I've always avoided organised structures, especially in my work; the institutions of the art and film world never attracted me; many of my friends 'played' the field but I kept apart.

You can't stand the virus up, if it makes you feel ill, you can't go out, and when you are ill in hospital you will be given a particular bed, where you will eat and sleep at a given time. How will you cope with that?
The hardest thing is not illness but the institutionalisation of cures.

Have you formulated a strategy?
No. I've chosen not to think of it, to put it in the back of my mind. I've never been interested in the future, only in the past insofar as it relates to the present. I can't waste time mulling over hypothetical scenarios. One might dream up an æsthetic exit and be caught short in an hotel room with ghastly wallpaper like Oscar Wilde.

If you can, trap me. I'll make a good patient because I was brought up in the environment of authority; it's going to be hard to pull me in though - I've been running all my life, playing truant. If you capture me I'll buckle down. I'll loathe you in secret and put on a good face.

And if you became ill do you think you'd manage?
My work is my life; I'd carry on working. I'm doing that now, turning the virus round. I have a vocation that comes before illness but I'm always trying to give it up. My motto is 'Silence is Golden' - but who lives up to their ideals? We are all failures and we know it. It's that knowledge which keeps us trying.

My father, who was quite like me, was finally laid low by a stroke. I'd never seen him so happy. He'd given up his role as the Air Commodore. Deprived of speech, in fact all communication, he just smiled.

How has your perspective changed? Do you think it will change further?
I'm on a see-saw, nothing has settled down. The virus elbowed it's way right into the centre of all our lives during this decade, rather like the new right that has infected British life. We heard the first rumours in the early eighties, by the Autumn of 1983 I had my first serious discussion about it with my friend Ron Wright in Berkeley. Ron told me how serious the

problem had become in San Francisco and he recommended that I stayed away from the bathhouses.

Then during 1984 the first of my friends died from pneumonia. No-one, not even the doctors, admitted he was a victim of the virus. One afternoon that same month I met Howard - who had left London over ten years before to live in Denmark; he looked a picture of health, tanned and smiling. 'How are you? You look great!' Since then I've learnt not to ask these questions on meeting anyone. He smiled - he had a very beautiful smile - and said, 'I have AIDS, Derek'. I tried to register no surprise. I didn't know what was expected. As we walked along he rolled up his shirtsleeves to show me his Kaposi; this was the first time I'd seen symptoms. We said goodbye at Cambridge Circus and never saw each other again.

Then it rollercoastered. The next month I met a film-maker in his early twenties out one evening. He looked terribly distressed, was drunk. He pulled me over and said, 'Derek, please help me. The doctor told me I had the virus and had six months to live. I've been walking around the streets since. I haven't been home. I don't know what to do. Can you help me tell my lover and my parents?'

I spent an anguished night with him making telephone calls.

Eventually, after I had taken him home, I walked back across London in a cold dawn. Slowly but surely every conversation and every encounter was stalked by the shadow of the virus; a terrible impotence overwhelmed us - there was nothing to do.

Almost monthly, one heard of a friend or acquaintance who was dying or dead; and still no information - just rumours. It was caused by amyl nitrate, by multiple sexual contacts, a mutation of syphilis or hepatitis; no-one knew.

Slowly, too slowly, our lives changed. It was as if the clock had been put into reverse, and then the EVIL began and I saw criminal newspapers like the *Sun* whip the flames - a paper which had the largest daily readership in Britain. These were the same people who'd waved the Nazis to victory in the thirties - they'd just mutated.

Some men were now literally on the run. The bombings began. You could feel the hatred in the eyes of the commuters.

Through good advice we stopped loving each other in the way we wished.

Adopted safe, then safer sex and then no sex at all. The gay community adjusted itself, funded the Terrence Higgins Trust; but still the vilification went on, even of those people who were hell-bent on educating us and saving lives. When they printed pamphlets and distributed them in the provinces, they were beaten up while the police stood by and laughed. A mad policeman called on God and described us as 'swirling in a cesspit'. By this time, it seemed that the world was literally taking leave of it's senses; the new right wallowed in the blood and unleashed Clause 28. Where do you think this will stop?

It has changed my perspective radically. I'd always been under the impression that Heterosoc was pretty dim. Now I know that I was right. Actively or through indifference they murdered us.

We were just watching the news about people dying on the tube at King's Cross. Death out of the blue is horrendous. Dying is, in a way, quite easy. If you are burnt to death in seconds - or even if you choke to death - then it's over quite quickly. HIV is very different.

At this moment, it hasn't caught up with me because I've buried myself in work, a way of coping with my situation. I've been working on the house and the garden here.
    I've watched people with a 'terminal' illness coping - my mother, for instance, who had cancer.

I am vain. The thought of being disfigured by the illness seems to me more horrendous than the illness itself. Perhaps I would gain the courage to go out and realise it wasn't so devastating. I feel marked out as a public person with HIV.

I would consider commiting suicide. I don't think I would find that difficult, although I've never contemplated it. I'm not too bothered about time; what do people do with the thirty minutes they save rushing about? Once you are dead, time telescopes - you'll all be there with me in the time it takes to boil a kettle.

Do you anticipate a sense of things being taken away?
No, just things I'd miss. I don't think that anyone would take anything

from me. If I was physically ill, I think I would make decisions. I'd carry on working, which is my life. If I couldn't make films I'd write, If I couldn't write I'd paint. I've always dreamt up things to do, I would find something which was within my capabilities.

What have you learnt so far?
I think I'm more self-contained this year than I have been and therefore more secure. My sexual drive is still there, although I do resent the fact that I've been forced into attempting a life of abstension.

The obvious next step is death.
I can't imagine that. I watched my mother die so I know what physical death is like, and I suspect that with variations it's more or less the same for us all.

In my mother's case they put her on a drug which made her very clear for a day but obviously overtaxed her system, as the next day she was unconscious. Speech became a whisper, like the twittering swallows which are the bird of death.

We all have to leave at some point but it's not the method I would have chosen. I console myself that maybe there is something good about going in three years, in my prime, at the height of my faculties, rather than declining to a sad old age.

Ten years ago, were you able to think about your own death?
Yes, all art is concerned with death: Goya, or those renaissance artists in their dissecting rooms; Rembrandt getting older in his self portraits; Monet's water lilies - which became the memorial for the first World War; the poetry of Wilfred Owen and Donne - *Death be not Proud*.
That's why I love Wilfred Owen - I feel a sympathy, it's just a different war.

Say you were struck down tomorrow, what would be your monument?
Oh nothing, because film disappears, thank God.

Is there not one statement that you would like to make?
I hope boys will carry on falling in love with boys and girls with girls, and *they'll* find no way to change that.

I'll have a state funeral, send all the boys to saunas, get them suntanned so they can march the streets of London quite naked, bronzed, and good-looking. Turn the House of Commons into a back-room for the under twenty-ones for a night.

I'll be cremated and have Christopher mix the ashes with black paint and paint five canvasses which I'll have signed - it'll be my last artwork. It seems to be a sensible way to deal with it, to become a work of art and retain some value in death.

* * *

Things turned out differently. I fell ill in February 1990, and until September that year spent most of my time in St. Mary's. I had TB of the liver, viral pneumonia, toxoplasmosis - which attacks the brain and blinds you - and some exploratory surgery which resulted in the removal of my appendix.

LAMENTATIONS

BILL GIBB

I never knew you were ill.

I woke up one December morning and saw headlines inches high in the *Sun* - you had died. Shocked.

They described you as a giant Scotsman. I don't remember you like that: a confident shyness, gentle-voiced, modest.

I still have a film of one of your shows years before.

After that we met on street corners in Soho - and now, when I turn the corner, there is one less surprise for me.

DAVID DIPNALL

When you died the future was young. Dark hair in a mop, broad faced with the smile of Puck, gold tooth glinting. Wotcher, wot yer doing mate?

No more concerts at the pub - bopping up and down like a demented American pilot. Fasten your seat-belts you're in for a bumpy ride. David who had more wild life in him.

Dartington, the Slade and death.

HOWARD BRUCKNER

We fucked in a backroom; that was wild. Of all my friends you were the greatest loss.

I understand the old rush to the grave when the laughter of a generation dies.

If I made my films for anyone it was for you, though you didn't know it. In Henry James's house in front of a winter fire the last time I saw you whole, you entertained us with magical stories.

I remember you in the video you made with Matt spoofing an epic Hollywood romance. Listening to the talking book with Madonna, Bob Wilson and William Burroughs - whose life you put so elegantly on film.

Before you died, I rang you in NYC, you had run out of words and your groans circled the world.

PAUL BETTELL

Gentle Paul Bettell, you made two gentle films and died so young.

They still play to rapt audiences in Berlin where HB carried you, dying, up some dozens of stairs into Tom's House.

When I first met you, you said, 'Derek please take me home, I can't possibly talk in this bar.' So we spent the night together talking of film between the sheets.

PAUL TREACY

I was transfixed by you on an August street, which was laughing with you wide-eyed - you were communicating by signing. You signed to me over the crowd and ended up teaching Spencer his part in my film *Caravaggio*. Working in the wardrobe, keeping everyone in stitches.

We never slept with each other, but you'd arrive at all odd hours and say, 'Let's have a quick one, Del boy'. I was ravished by you and then you left, skeletal, on crutches, over the shingle at Dungeness. I was heartbroken.

ROBERT FRASER

Sitting in Bar Italia wrapped against the cold and illness, uncomplaining. You first crossed swords with them when the *News of the World* destroyed your glittering life, acting as *agents provocateurs* to have you and Mick Jagger arrested; my friend Richard immortalised that in art.

Swingeing London. I demonstrated for you in the streets the night they snuffed out your bright-minded gallery.

My friend Nina sent you to India; you came back with Keralese dancers to pick up the threads, but it was never quite the same.

You gave Keith Haring an exhibition and then you both left us.

ROBERT MAPPLETHORPE

Robert 'who cares a fuck about photos' - they came two days after we rushed into bed. Flesh was your passion, not the silvery prints.

I sat at a table when you hustled Sam who had 'discovered' photography then discovered you.

Then you hustled your way right out of my life, but, passing me as the dawn broke over Heaven, you said, 'I have gotten everything I ever wished for. What did you get, Derek?'

TERRY LEAR

Strong and tall with tight curly blonde hair and a broad smile, you wished to become a pop star; but at 25 in your washed-out blue jeans as blue as your blue blue eyes you were struck down. Incontinent, stuck in a chair, you waited so long to die, and you died in such anguish.

You used to come in your Summer's lunch-break. 'Let's have a good laugh,' you'd say, unbuttoning those Levis.

Big-hearted, I filmed you against a sky-blue wall, you danced like a boxer, pushing your fist at the lens, always laughing.

PLUS AND MINUS

Did you see the announcement of your HIV status as a political act?
Yes I did; but it was politics in the first person. All the information I was receiving then counteracted the way I felt.

In 1986, being tested was such an issue. Before I made a film, I had to pass a medical for insurance; would I have to lie about that? I lied to the U.S. immigration - it is illegal to enter America with HIV. Within days, my own personal insurance and integrity was questioned.

I was always bad with secrets. I made the decision to get tested; all the other steps came from that. I wasn't sensational about it. Nicholas de Jongh wrote about it as an aside in the *Guardian*. I thought that was the best way of dealing with it - we organised it together.

It became more difficult when the tabloids moved in - it took about two years for that. I wasn't a pop or film star, if I had been it would have been an overnight sensation, like Rock Hudson.

The virus was now central to my life. I came to terms with it on so many different levels, both personal and public. I had to keep filming. Was I uninsurable? Friends? Painting? Writing? Making *The Garden*? The pressures were affecting the way I thought and the way I conducted my life; there isn't a day I'm not under assault. How to survive as a reasonably intact human being undamaged by popular preconceptions and misconceptions? It has been a long uphill battle. I would see the steps being made by people who were much better informed than myself in health education and other areas, debating on television; the next time you saw the debate it had gone back to square one - like learning your alphabet again.

Every time I met a journalist I had to start from scratch, because I couldn't be certain that any of the information that had been put out had reached them. People had a way of protecting themselves from this information - they didn't want to know. It's still the same: it's rare to meet a journalist from the national press who has any knowledge of the problems of being HIV+.

The British press has an obsession with you - you are probably one of the most quoted artists today - yet there seems to be this frustration.
Well, I haven't died. There's a frustration on both our parts that I

haven't. I want out of all of this - to put an end to it because it's so aggravating; I feel I've done everything an individual could do. I'm fed up with the sound of my voice. Then another paper comes with readers who haven't read the last; well, maybe I can help; my mail would seem to suggest it.

I've had all the opportunistic infections. I've strung them round my neck like a necklace of pearls - and survived them. The reviews of the films as 'another death work by Derek' began to look a bit silly.

What happens if you survive?
Many people died quickly through fear and medical ignorance. That's changed. I feel that, if I can recover once, there's no reason why I can't recover again. When I came down with PCP, I went into hospital, and put on my 'I'm-going-to-be-out-in-two-week's-time-pyjamas' - that's how I've treated it.

The Garden *has been cited as an elegiac film.*
I felt elegiac making it, I built the garden and then sat there wondering whether I would be there next year to enjoy it. Two years ago, I wound up my life, wrote a will, and gave all my writing to the film archive.

I cleared up the house so that other people wouldn't have the problem. It was easy to say to the film archive, 'Come and take everything but you've got to take it by next Thursday'. I had a three week period when I put my affairs in order, or was it disorder?

Were you a victim of HIV propaganda yourself?
Yes, Chris, we all are; no-one isn't affected. At first because several of my dearest friends died. When I was diagnosed five years ago, I thought I would be around for two or three years; that's the time you were given; that changed.

I was ill in hospital for half a year. I began to experience the parameters of therapy, which is something you can read about but which is very different experienced.

I've never been involved in 'alternative' medicine; that is alright if you're well. It can put you into the right frame of mind - so I'm for it. On the other hand if you're dealing with an infection like TB, then I don't think the Bach Flower Remedy is going to work. You're down with a temperature of 103° or 104°, sweating it out for weeks and you've lost three stone in weight - you're very happy when someone gives you Ritafer that clears it up.

There are mental and psychological defences; looking back it was unpleasant at the time, but it feels worse now than it was when it was happening.

Are you subverting a propaganda?

I am involved as one body. My experience and yours may be different. It was a minefield to be one of the few identifiable HIV+ men in the world, realising that whatever I said might be taken as representative. My age, experience, work, were all different. The pressures of HIV are as numerous as the people who have to cope with them.

I was never given an analytical education. I am an artist who worked from enthusiasms and worked out enthusiasms. I never thought through what the HIV announcement would cost me. Like most of us in the eighties, I was fairly ostrich-like. Friends of mine were much more aware of the outcome.

In *Dancing Ledge*, which I wrote in 1982-83, there's a mention of HIV which gives you the theories of that time - conspiracy theories - and I suggest that prudence is a good thing rather than abstention. I was dismayed that another generation might be denied the marvellous free-wheeling time we had. I was dismayed by those who said monogamy was the coming thing - just what we fought against. The great value about being Queer was that you could join a group. Anyone could be in it. It was a support system.

One of the most interesting letters I received about my book *Modern Nature* was from woman of sixty-nine. She had noticed what a caring group of people were around me, something she lacked as a heterosexual; she felt she was much more isolated than I.

MY MOUTH IS OPEN AND MY BODY IS IN PRISON

Neither of the lads I spoke to on the Heath were the sort I'd expect to find in a bar. The young Liverpudlian said: 'I can cope with the cold. I have to. I can't afford to put the heating on, so I crawl between the sheets and watch television.' His mate said: 'Well, at least you've got a television to watch. Maybe you could invite me round more often so I could watch it too.'

There's an amazing amount of pretence we go through to meet people in public spaces; the drinks you have to buy, the smoke and noise. On the Heath you can be stone cold sober and meet someone; in the bars you are obliged to drink.

How did you feel about the sex?
It was liberating. It liberated me in a moment from the censure and five years of self-denial. I used every excuse for my problems, but the real problem was that I had been hemmed in. I saw my friend Andrew and talked to him about our situation. He said thank God you're talking to me because you are the only person who can get through; not even an analyst can break through with advice because they can't understand this. My mouth is open but my body is in prison. Everyone I meet up there is involved in this battle, even if they don't know it.

First of all, we have been turned into the people who have to bear all the responsibility. We have to bear the responsibility for the epidemic, for educating people. Then we have to act responsibly while they do nothing. How can the ignorant speak so coldly in the newspapers? Naïve, self-congratulating and deluded, they want to foist their vulgarity on the rest of us.

We live in a situation where few speak up. There have been so few voices from the epidemic. They are generally wheeled on at the end of a chapter, 'Oh, ANON. is HIV+' and they're blanked out, you see the silhouette of a head in the darkness and they are given their three minutes, if they're lucky - cut off quickly if they get boring. I haven't seen many faces like Johnny Grimshaw who was the first to come out in public as HIV+.

It's not good television, is it?
I tried to open a debate. I don't think we can expect any solutions or resolutions - I don't believe in that. But when people talk we return to sanity.

You could go to any straight pub and put yourself at risk a hundred times. That's what happens on Saturday night; straight boys don't put on condoms - it makes them Queer. On the Heath, I think most people know the parameters.

I was in love with all those boys and I wasn't going to have their passion trashed by evil people. That's what love's about. I'm a passionate militant. If I wanted to kill someone, I wouldn't do it on the Heath. I'd go with a machetti to a newspaper office like my father on his fucking bomber raids. If my father could bomb the Nazis, get away with it, and become a hero, why couldn't I bludgeon them? Nazism was a state of mind - they were all around us.

I bubble with anger underneath. It's maddening. I wish I didn't.

Really?
I don't think anger is the best motivation, although it is essential if you're going to change anything.

What would you do without your anger?
Probably nothing.

Is there an element of madness to your anger?
Yes, I am quite mad! All artists are - divine madness. Pasolini was as mad as a hatter. When I met him I recognised that part of myself.

LOVE ME TENDER, FUCK ME TOO

Cruising Hampstead Heath has frightened them, suddenly Derek's a bad boy again.
They accepted me as long as I carried the scourge of a generation. Now people were saying: 'He's not such a bad person really and you wouldn't wish the AIDS on anyone'. What a laugh! There I was being as responsible as possible, but there was one flaw - people were not prepared to look a Queer fuck in the face.

When I wrote *Modern Nature*, Shaun, who edited it, took out the pieces on Hampstead Heath; he said he thought it was a byway and it diverted from the book. HB insisted on re-instating them and I agreed with him. I wasn't expecting them to be taken out.

I always went to the Heath from the moment my friend Michael told me about it in the sixties. It's completely Queer, rooted in sex - a completely Queer space. Few people fuck there any longer, but there is choice. All you can do is to give everyone the information. They have to make their own decisions. For instance, if you decide to fuck me without a condom and I consent, where does responsibility lie? People are responsible for themselves.

Is there anything you are afraid of?
Myself. Up to this moment I have been open, but there is a side of me that wishes I hadn't - that's the part of me that I'm frightened of.

What do you mean?
My whole being wants to jettison this baggage - all the safer sex advice, the condoms and everything else. Isn't that the same for all of us? Why should anyone who hasn't been tested behave differently?

Remember, my generation became infected through lack of knowledge and the next will become infected through lack of information.

Do you care?
I do, I don't. It's double edged. I care a lot.

Do you?
Oh, fuck it!

SAFER SEX

It was raining. I left you in the pub, wrapped myself up and took off.

There were a dozen or more people up there, everyone standing around. I had been there about twenty minutes when I noticed a young man. He was wearing a jacket with a crazy design on the back. I went up to him and he threw his arms around me. It was electric. We had the wildest time. I got a hard-on for the first time in years. He went crazy for this. It was very sexy. At some point, out of breath, he came. I walked after him thinking what am I going to say to break into his silence?

I tapped him on the shoulder, 'Are you Tony?' I had found a message in my back jean pocket which said *My name is Tony and I live in a hotel and it's safe and you're welcome and the bus routes are...*

'No I'm not. Why did you ask me that?'

'I don't know, It's just that I thought you might be Tony.'

He said, 'Well, that's a strange thing,' and stopped. We started to talk; we had been having such a good time, then this man came up and said 'Hello Steve,' and he said, 'Oh, hello Tony.' The man said, 'It's fucking awful. I've been putting these messages in pockets and no-one ever rings up.' I said 'Well, Tony, I rang you!'

'Who are you?'

'I'm the one who rang you up and said I lived in the country'.

He was gobsmacked! My friend said to me, 'Let's go, he's crazy'.

We started to have sex again. I put a condom into his hand and he fucked me really well. When it was over, he took this condom off and it went 'snap!' in the night and he came all over the place.

'That's the best thing that's happened to me for such a long time,' I said.

'Yeah, I know.'

We chatted for twenty minutes or so and walked back to the car park before parting company.

'I'm going to have to explain why I've got muddy feet again!' he said.

'Doesn't he know you come up here?'

'No, he doesn't. I've lived near the Heath for a year or two and I often come down, usually very early in the morning before I go to work. There's always some last person here, usually they're elderly and cold and I brew up some coffee and bring it down for them in a flask.'

As I left him I told him we are all going to be old some day.

HOW THE KISS OF DEATH
BECAME THE KISS OF LIFE

1) A local authority shall not:

   a) Intentionally promote homosexuality or publish material with the intention of promoting homosexuality.

   b) Promote the teaching in any maintained school of the accept-

ability of homosexuality as a pretended family relationship.
2) Nothing in subsection 1 shall be taken to prohibit the doing of any thing for the purpose of treating or preventing the spread of disease.
3) In any proceedings in connection with the application of this sec tion a court shall draw such inferences as to the intention of the local authority as may reasonably be drawn from the evidence before it.

— SECTION 28, LOCAL GOVERNMENT ACT 1988

As you celebrated Christmas 1987, we were under attack by the only western government in recent history to introduce legislation increasing prejudice. The Clause would have liked to have stamped us out, grind us down, the kiss of death. Herod run rampant amongst the homo inno-cents.

But up went a chorus, 'enough is enough'. Thousands marched in the streets, protests in every city, abseiling dykes, riots at the edge of Downing Street, Sue Lawley cowering whilst handcuffed lesbians screamed 'STOP THE CLAUSE' on the Six o' Clock News.

What had begun to look like a moribund movement full of political die-hards, bitter infighting and bar banter, woke up. The kiss of death became the kiss of life - a new lesbian and gay movement emerged, stronger than ever, more angry, more focussed.

Four times in 1988 we broke the record for Europe's largest Queer demo - 12,000; 15,000; 20,000; 25,000. We learnt who our true allies were, and our fair-weather friends. The Labour Party deserted us at the first hurdle, the *Guardian* told us that Clause 28 was our own fault. The Clause became law - plays banned, exhibitions stopped, teachers silenced. But for what?

Happy Christmas, Margaret.

1990s

A SAINT IN DUNGENESS

PRESS RELEASE
immediate - immediate - immediate

Film director Derek Jarman will be canonised as a saint by the gay order of nuns, the Sisters of Perpetual Indulgence, at his famous garden in Dungeness, Kent. This is in recognition of his films and books, for all he does for the lesbian and gay community, and because 'he has a very sexy nose'.

The ceremony takes place on Sunday, 22nd September 1991. The ritual includes a procession, the hymn Amazing Pride, *a laying on of hands and a mass communion. Derek Jarman will be crowned with a saint's halo, appropriately woven of celluloid film. He will be titled 'Saint Derek of Dungeness of the Order of Celluloid Knights'.*

The Sisters of Perpetual Indulgence are a worldwide order of gay nuns, whose mission is to expiate homosexual guilt from all and to replace it with universal joy. The London Chapter now celebrate their first anniversary, are 20 in number, and houses of nuns are being established in Canterbury and Leeds. Their titles include Sister Jack-Off All Trade, Sister Dominatrix, and Mother Care and Control.

The Sisters have created saints worldwide to recognise those who have achieved and struggled for the lesbian and gay community. These include Australian saints who have worked for gay prisoners' rights, for anti-discrimination legislation and on gay radio.

The Sisters say, 'Pope John Paul II has created 234 new saints, at the rate of 19 a year, so it's time we started.'

* * *

It's no small thing to be made a saint, especially when you're alive and kicking and have to give your consent. In spite of the Sisters' warning not to let it go to my head, I had to take it seriously. I am, after all, the first Kentish saint since Queer Thomas of Canterbury who was murdered by his boyfriend, Henry, in 1170.

Eileen in the Light Railway Café asked, 'Why are you being made a saint?' 'Fate!?' I answered. The local billboards proclaimed 'SAINT IN DUNGENESS' and now mail arrives addressed to 'The Saint'.

It's 22nd December 1991, the grim anniversary of my discovery that I was HIV positive. I am expecting a Japanese girl who has flown all the way from Tokyo.

On the Saint's Day, the sun came out and the wind got up, blowing the habits of the sisters like flags this way and that, and a congregation of a hundred people arrived from here and there to rehearse the order of service in high Palace by Sister Celebrant, Mother Fecundity of the Mass Uprising.

I dithered about my costume like any old queen off to a ball. Should I be plain ordinary Joe Saint or something a little more glittering? I gave in to temptation and chose the sparkling golden robe that Steven had worn as Edward II in the film.

⁂ ⁂ ⁂

Sister Celebrant: How bona to vada your dolly old eeks.
Sisters: Bona to vada you.
Gathered Faithful: To vada you bona.

The gathered faithful will sing:

ALL NUNS BRIGHT AND BEAUTIFUL

chorus
All Nuns bright and beautiful,
All Sisters great and small.
All Nuns wise and wonderful,
Come join us, hear the call.

1.
Each queen free of the closet,
Each dyke found free of shame
Lives life with gay abandon,
And takes no guilt or blame.

2.
It's easy with a Sister,
We don't take shock or flight.
Though sometimes our communion,
Goes on throughout the night.

After singing the hymn *Amazing Pride*, the service ended; we all had tea in the garden and went down to the sea.

I'm alone again. I sit watching the sun go down, peach as my grandmother's table-cloth behind the nuclear power station. A great orange moon hangs over the sea and the winds die bringing in the night.

LOVE

Everyone suddenly burst out singing;
And I was filled with such delight
As prisoned birds must find in freedom,
Winging wildly across the white
Orchards and dark-green fields; on - on - and out of sight.

Everyone's voice was suddenly lifted;
And beauty came like the setting sun:
My heart was shaken with tears; and horror
Drifted away... O, but Everyone
Was a bird; and the song was wordless; and the singing will never be done.

Siegfried Sassoon's poem was written at the end of the First World War.

I am tired tonight. My eyes are out of focus, my body droops under the weight of the day, but as I leave you Queer lads let me leave you singing. I had to write of a sad time as a witness - not to cloud your smiles - please read the cares of the world that I have locked in these pages; and after, put this book aside and love. May you of a better future, love without a care and remember we loved too. As the shadows closed in, the stars came out.

I am in love.

While I was writing this book, I was in touch with friends who are involved in the struggle for civil rights. Many of them sent me information and the best way to include it was to publish what they had written.

an appendix

HETERO HERO AND HOMO WEIRDO
A Tabloid Monologue
Pascal Brannan, November 1991

Magic Johnson - heterosexual, Afro-American major league basketball player, announces that he has the virus HIV and the next day the President of the United States congratulates him as an all-American Hero and offers him a place on the National AIDS Committee.

This week on Saturday, Freddie Mercury - lead singer with the band 'Queen', born Fredrick Bulsara in Madagascar - released a statement indicating that he has the virus HIV. The next day, twenty four hours later, Freddie Mercury has died from AIDS and the tabloids heave into action.

There is Mary, a platonic girlfriend of many long years standing. The *Daily Mirror* runs a caption next to her tear-stained face, *So Close to Mary Yet So Many Gay Affairs,* and again one more innocent Mary is dragged forward to play the tabloid victim. A subsequent paragraph tells of Freddie's generosity. Or at least the first sentence reveals that Mercury had bought up several mansions for friends. The next ten started with the word 'but' and were devoted to tales of Freddie 'The Bitch'. A lover kicked out from FM's Mercedes onto a deserted stretch of German Autobahn for having changed channels on the car's on-board TV set without asking the Royal Queen's approval. The shocking thing for me was the realisation that the vehicle was stationary at the time. Poor Freddie was miffed. I'm not surprised.

A pop star announces that Freddie was 'really' camp. Really? Darling, Freddie Mercury was the biggest fucking queen on God's earth. The most gorgeous, enormous, wildest fucking queen who fucked them all off in dying from AIDS.

Mercury's sexuality was supposedly his secret, as was his race, colour and creed. White, European rock fans - heterosexual, of course - have rested easy with the idea that Freddie Mercury was the King of Queen. Theatrically seen to exist alongside heterosexuality. No longer.

The King is dead, long live the Queen.

The latest videos from Queen, filmed on blockbuster budgets, focus on the great queen of Queen careering about with a whitened face and a bunch of bananas on his head. This is not simply some theatrical device, but a wan, worn, Carmen Miranda escaping into one last manic aria. The titles of these latest songs include *The Show Must Go On, I'm Going Slightly Mad.* Slightly mad? AIDS induced senile dementia no doubt and Mr. and Mrs. Heterosexual sit back to enjoy. Whilst homosexuals die, many heterosexuals reach for the remote control and simply turn up the volume. Does it come in stereo?

We are not allowed to grieve. Elton John's floral tribute and the message attached, photographed and splashed across the tabloids. Are we saddened at the loss of a friend or fear only that we might be next? Heterosexuals in their discomfort of any display of emotion between men implicate a simple expression of love with their own fearful concerns.

One can not but admire Magic Johnson in revealing to the American public that he was HIV positive. Especially as he did so in such a public manner. American news features carried the words 'condom', 'penis' and 'vagina' all in the same sentence and on prime-time television. One can only wish him health and happiness and the strength to withstand the media bashing he is already having to endure; but, one cannot help but agree with the recently politicised Martina Navratilova, who declared on hearing the news that if it had been a straight woman, or a gay man revealing that they had HIV they would be met with much less a hero's welcome.

Anger and hostility, snide subterfuge and a great deal of pious finger wagging. The illness is less important than appropriating blame, if blame were there.

Robert Maxwell died recently too, the owner of the *Daily Mirror.* A large and portly man, or as the *Mirror* itself might say, as fat as a whale and as big as three buses, fell from his yacht and drowned having suffered a massive coronary. The man dies from a heart attack and we are given a detailed description of his last supper; grouse stuffed with baby asparagus, and a bottle of claret.

When I go, I hope to be remembered with as much affection, my nose buried up some charming young man's arsehole, a bottle of poppers in one hand and his large cock in the other.

Living life to the full, the tabloid headlines will run, *he died from AIDS.*

Not weird but Queer.

PS. As a footnote I read that FM's lover, Jim, a burly hairdresser from Dublin, will inherit some of Freddie's many millions. Another of Freddie's secrets - the lover, not the money. His existence denied although present at the funeral. His grief is hidden from us still.

THE EVENING'S STANDARDS

Only two reviews of *Edward* have talked of me as if I was dead. The most surprising, Alex Walker in the *Standard*:

The *Evening Standard*, 17/10/91

> *Derek Jarman's* Edward II *seeks to reclaim English history for the Outrage campaign and present homosexuality as the driving force behind social repression in modern as well as medieval England.*
>
> *Like the director, himself, these days, the movie possesses a strong streak of wishful martyrdom. I think it's getting on people's nerves to hear Jarman advertising himself - or being advertised - in every branch of the media as the most famous living HIV positive victim, but there's no doubt the dying fall that the unfortunately stricken film-maker deliberately emphasises in his version of Marlowe's play gives it a terminal power.*
>
> *Without this, it would simply be a campy re-working of the story about the sodomite sovereign and his catamite court favourite (Steven Waddington and Andrew Tiernan respectively, but hard to tell apart sometimes as each is a redhead and has gone to the same crimper).*
>
> *Apart from the view of Britain as a repressive society bent on sending every gay in the land to the Clause 28 death camp, the movie's main*

message is that love of boys far transcends the love of women. It always did in Jarman's œuvre. But this time at least he's got textual authority for his misogyny, though I think he pushes it even farther than Marlowe by presenting Edward's treacherous Queen Isabella (Tilda Swinton) as a Vampyra-like zombie who goes literally for the jugular at the cocktail hour and sinks her teeth in the neck of the king's disloyal brother (Jerome Flynn).

Sandy Powell has costumed the predominantly male cast in a range of modern menswear that runs from Commes des Garçons-like suits to SAS camouflage uniforms while passing through the wardrobe racks of glad (or gay) rags like the leopard skin bathrobe modelled by the homophobic Lord Mortimer (Nigel Terry, almost the only one of the cast able, or perhaps caring, to speak Marlowe's poetry with any metrical fluency).

What saves the movie from the stiff monotony of its endless little tableaux is the feeling it builds up of England as a paranoid pressure-chamber whose repressiveness leads to demos in the streets with Gaveston being crushed to death between police riot shields. The law is presented as a lackey of state facism, a rather extreme view even for those who cruise on Hampstead Heath.

Jarman deconstructs the tragedy in order to re-invent it as a series of revue sketches (king and favourite, clad in Marks and Spencers pyjamas, dancing together to Annie Lennox's version of Cole Porter's Ev'ry Time We Say Goodbye), Brechtian agitprop (a board meeting of Moral Majority Ltd) or simply "good idea at the time" interludes (a rugby scrum whose nude players seem to have left their strip in the changing room).

Oddly for a film that flies the colours of Jarman's queer nation, it is short on visibly erotic energy. The pumping rumps of the rough trade are almost lethargically put on show. Even the king's crush on his own kind is compromised by being presented as if homosexual love were the second best thing if you can't rise to the demands of the heterosexual kind. When it came to being bent, Marlowe at least played it straight.

Co-financed by the Japanese, the film in a sort of sandbox furnished with a spare selection of props, court flunkeys like the wind-up dolls and a waterhole in which Edward, for no obvious reason, is occasionally discovered standing and drooling about his lover. It has a certain kabuki-like spookiness that will probably go over big in the East. But for me, the movie testifies more to Jarman's strengths (public provocation) and weaknesses (indiscriminate puerility) than any film he has made.

JARMAN, AIDS AND THE VIRUS OF PREJUDICE
The *Evening Standard*, 23/10/91

Your film critic Alexander Walker is entitled to his professional view of Derek Jarman's new film, Edward II. However, I object to his personal remarks claiming that the director is "advertising himself - or being advertised in every branch of the media as the most famous living HIV positive victim" (sic) and referring to him as "stricken" and possessing a "strong streak of wishful martyrdom".

Derek Jarman has always been controversial and addresses himself enthusiastically. That he has not chosen to hide his HIV status is characteristic of his honesty and his willingness to help foster more sensible attitudes to HIV.

That this has sometimes led to a certain voyeurism on the media about this tremendously alive man and his virus is an expression of the problem he seeks to resolve. It is unjust to blame him for it.
Like any artist in the public eye, of course he must advertise his work, and it is by his work he should be assessed, not by his virus.

His open approach to life is a beacon to anyone, HIV positive or negative. Holding the benefit premiere for our AIDS research programme was characteristically generous, but in no way self-serving.

It was sad indeed that a respected critic should display such an unfair and negative view of Derek Jarman as a person, in a way that seemed gratuitously hurtful.

People living with HIV and AIDS and those working with them look forward to the day when such attitudes, and the distorted values they reflect, are consigned to history.

- Anthony Pinching, Reader in Clinical Immunology, St Mary's Hospital Medical School, Paddington W2.

A BEACON FOR GAY PROMISCUITY
The *Evening Standard*, 30/10/91

I wonder if Dr Anthony Pinching, reader in clinical immunology, would have a word with Derek Jarman and persuade him to put to good use his "willingness to help foster more sensible attitudes to HIV".

I did not detect much of this willingness when I read Jarman's recent diary, Modern Nature, *where he gives the promiscuously gay "and brave" encouragement for a nights' revelry on Hampstead Heath between 10.30pm and 3am. "Sex on the heath is an idyllic free fall... all the Cains and Abels you could wish for are out on a hot night".*

Is this what Dr Pinching means by Jarman's "open approach to life (which) is a beacon for anyone, HIV positive or negative?"

- Alexander Walker, St Johns Wood, NW8

AIDS AND PREJUDICE
The *Evening Standard*, 4/11/91

Sex on the Heath is as safe as Sex on the Hearth

Alexander Walker's attack on me in his review of my film of Edward II, *and his criticism of Dr Anthony Pinching is both naïve and ill-mannered. I suggest he give up film reviewing for a week or so and research the HIV epidemic if he wants to be involved. The first lesson he will learn is that HIV is not linked to promiscuity (one more person than you are prepared to sleep with) if safer sex practices, which are widely known by gay men and ill publicised in the straight press, are adhered to. Who is he, who neither states his HIV status nor sexual preferences, to criticise the right of myself or any PWA to have sex. The precautions we take are our affair. Moral censure will not solve the problem. Open discussions will do more good. I could have taken the diary entries from* Modern Nature *out, my editor wished me to do so, but I replaced them to open debate not close doors. If he thinks that being open about my HIV status was a pecadillo in the climate fostered by remarks like this, he should think harder.*

Finally, I find it offensive to have critics continually harping on about my mortality. It is possible to be a person living with AIDS, it is also possible to survive owing to the dedicated research of men like Anthony Pinching. This survival is what hurts the censorious the most.

- Derek Jarman, Charing Cross Road, WC2.

underlined excerpts of the original letter were not included in the published copy.

FROM A FLYER PICKED UP AT HEAVEN,
October 1991

Haven't we had enough of the lies being peddled by our 'leaders'? By our 'gay' press? By 'gay' Mafia like Stonewall & GALOP? By gay bars & clubs which are run by exploiting straights who rip off our culture? By 'lesbian' & 'gay' censors who try to control our lives by controlling our images? By political parties, who with fools like McKellen are trying to shut us up? Buy our VOTES, our MINDS, our BODIES!

IT'S TIME TO FIGHT Time to take our anger out of the clubs & bars, cottages & cruising grounds, & onto the streets. Time to show the Majors & Kinnocks of this country that we can't be BOUGHT. It's time to put our COCKS & CUNTS on the line, to smash once & for all the lie that we're all the same, that we want to be like the gay & straight zombies out there who watch PROPAGANDA TV, who believe the lies in the *Sun* & the *Guardian*, who think they've a right to judge us, our bodies, our lovers, our lives, who think they hold some moral highground! They're selling us out. Confining us to monogamy, marriage, & mortgage!

It's time to SMASH once & for all the myth of the 'gay' community, which allows fools like the Stonewall Group & *Capital Gay* to sell us out, to sell our souls to the devils of straight culture. They're trying to put us on that Titanic, and we're sitting idly by!

Queers, start speaking for yourself! Queers, Dykes, Fags, Fairies, Arse-bandits, Drag Queens, Trannies, Clubbers, Sluts. It doesn't matter what you call yourself - you know who you are. Don't let assimilationists kid you with their patronising crap about the oppression of language. Call yourself what you want. Reject all labels. Liberate yourself from the lie that we're all lesbians & gay men. Free yourself from the lie that we're all the same.

For years we've been fed the lie that our sexuality is based on the gender of the person we sleep with. We've trapped ourselves into a GHETTO of our own making. It's time to turn on our oppressors, gay & straight, who try to control us.

QUEER means to fuck with gender. Our sexuality is unique. It's not about whether you fuck with boys or girls. Are you into tall or short, black or white, old or young, fisting or fucking, thin or fat, drugs, SM or vanilla? Do you gobble it up or spit it out? Does she come all over you? Do you push him up against the wall & fuck him? Are you playing safe?

LIBERATE YOUR MINDS
QUEER IS NOT ABOUT GAY OR LESBIAN - IT'S ABOUT SEX

There are straight Queers, bi Queers, tranny Queers, lez Queers, fag Queers, SM Queers, fisting Queers in every single street in this apathetic country of ours. We are everywhere. It's time to take it into the streets. Get out there! Take them on! Be yourself! And if you don't like this, get out and make some NOISE yourself. Write books. Be safe. Burn buildings. Shoot closets. Screw in the streets.

NO ASSIMILATION.
NO LIES.
NO SELL OUT.
NO LEADERS.
NO TRUTH.
NO PRISONERS.

144

CRIMINAL INJUSTICE
Peter Tatchell, November 1991

Ninety-six years after the trail of Oscar Wilde, the anti-gay laws which led to the imprisonment of one of the greatest writers of the nineteenth century are still on the statute books. Every year, thousands of men continue to be prosecuted for victimless gay behaviour. Despite moves towards closer integration with Europe, Britain still sanctions a level of institutionalised judicial discrimination against its gay and bisexual citizens which is far greater than any other European Community member state.

My own recent research, based on official Home Office figures, has shown that in England and Wales during 1989, consenting homosexual relations between men over the age of 16 resulted in:

- 3,500 prosecutions.
- 2,700 convictions and 380 cautions.
- 40 - 50 prison sentences.

Among those victimised were 31 men age 21 or over who were gaoled for consensual gay acts with other men aged 16 - 21. Dozens of teenagers were also penalised: 185 were convicted, 147 cautioned and 23 imprisoned for the predominantly gay consensual offences of buggery, soliciting, indecency and procuring. These prosecutions of teenagers make a mockery of the government's claim that Britain's harsh anti-gay laws exist to 'protect' young people. If that's the case why are these teenagers being prosecuted?

In 1989 the criminalisation of men for consenting gay behaviour cost the tax payer:
- £12 million for 3,500 prosecutions.
- £1 million for the imprisonment of 40 - 50 men.

This squandering of public money on the prosecution and punishment of gay men for victimless acts comes at a time when most police forces are facing budget crises, and when thousands of serious violent crimes (including queer-bashings) are being left unsolved.

Anti-gay bias within the criminal justice system is indicated by the following evidence from the government's criminal statistics for 1989:
- 30% of all gay sex convictions are for consensual gay behaviour (though this behaviour compromises only 13% of recorded sex offences).

● Men who commit consenting homosexual acts are four times more likely to be convicted than men who commit heterosexual and violent sex offences.

● The average police clear-up rate for the mainly consensual gay offences of buggery, procuring, and indecency is 97%, which is 28% higher than the average clear-up rate for rape and indecent assault on a woman. This extraordinarily high clear-up rate for victimless homosexual offences is suggestive of a police vendetta against the gay community.

● Compared with men who have consenting sex with girls under 16, men who commit the consensual offence of 'indecency between males' with partners over 16 are five times more likely to be prosecuted, and three times less likely to get off with a caution.

● Convictions for victimless homosexual indecency rose by 106% between 1985-'89. According to the Home Office this can be explained by the decision of some Chief Constables to 'target' these offences. Comparable heterosexual behaviour is rarely, if ever, targeted by the police.

● As a result, the number of convictions for consenting homosexual indecency was nearly four times greater in 1989 that in 1966 - the year before the ostensible decriminalisation of male homosexuality.

● Men who have consenting sex with 13 - 16 year old boys nearly always get charged with 'indecent assault' (despite the boys being willing participants); whereas an 'indecent assault' charge is almost never brought against men who have consensual sex with girls in the same age range.

● Prison sentences for consenting homosexual relations with men aged 16 - 21 are sometimes as long as for rape, and are often twice as long as the gaol terms for 'unlawful sexual intercourse' with a girl aged 13 - 16.

This homophobia of the British legal system is increasingly out of step with the rest of Europe. Last year, for example, newly-democratic Czechoslovakia lowered the age of consent for lesbians and gay men to 15; thereby ensuring parity with the age of consent for heterosexuals. In Britain, however, we continue to have more laws against gay sex than any other country in Europe, East or West. We also prosecute more men for consenting homosexual behaviour than any other European nation.

With 1992 on the horizon, now is the time to campaign for 'Equality with Europe'. As Britain joins the process of closer European integration, lesbians and gay men have a right to expect European standards of equality. That means an equal age of consent for everyone, including homo-sexuals (16 like the Netherlands); partnership rights for couples of the same sex (as in Denmark); anti-discrimination legislation to outlaw job refusals and dismissals (similar to France); and laws against incitement to hatred to stop anti-gay abuse (along the lines of Ireland). Nothing would better commemorate the centenary of Oscar Wilde's trial in 1995 than the repeal of Britain's anti-gay laws and the achievement of full equality for the lesbian and gay citizens of this country.

1989 is the latest year for which full information is published. The figures quoted are based on official Home Office statistics for the offences of soliciting, buggery, procuring and indecency (plus estimates of indecency offences under bye-laws etc. which are not listed in the official figures). Since some of these offences occasionally involve heterosexual behaviour, coercion or youngsters under 16, such cases have been subtracted from the total to produce the quoted figures for consenting homosexual behaviour with men over the age of 16.

COPPING OUT? THE POLITICS OF QUEER POLICING
Paul Burston, December 1991

Can't you just be homo without being so sexual? A question which has dominated my relations with *heterosocials* for longer than I care to remember. *Why do gay men always have to talk about sex?* Perhaps because my sexual preference is what marks me out, not simply as differ-ent, but as deviant. And even as they're launching into the usual kindly lesson on why I should resist defining myself according to my difference *for my own good,* my attention is elsewhere, recollecting the man who called me at work today because he'd been arrested in a public toilet, or the boy who'd been queerbashed by a gang of thugs on a common some-where, and was afraid of reporting the attack for fear of recrimination - *What were you doing there? Are you aware that this is a place frequented by homosexuals?*

It's no accident that for much of the past two years gay campaigning energies have been focussed on our relationship with the police. (And there is a relationship there, whether we choose to recognise it or not). It is the police, more so than any other public institution, who determine the exact extent of our liberation. Socially disenfranchised by an Act of Parliament which tolerates us as *homos* but only suffers our *sexuality* under prescribed conditions, location is the key, not only to our respectability, but to our criminality. (Let's not forget Lord Arran's warning to us in 1967, that we show our gratitude by comporting ourselves 'quietly and with dignity'). The Tory government's misanthropic attempt to privatise homosexuality under Section 28 was of minor consequence compared to the extensive and (let's hand it to them) highly imaginative measures adopted by Her Majesty's constabulary for the regulation of our desire. Consigned to preserve the boundary between public and private life, policing has always been a political activity, and in no case more conspicuously than ours. A criminal record as a sex offender is still a high price to pay for being caught with your trousers down.

That said, are we to conclude, as some would suggest, that the police are puppets of a Tory conspiracy, helpfully decked out in tell-tale blue, programmed to persecute us at any given opportunity? However chic it may be to wear allegations of recriminalisation on your chest, the simple fact remains that we were never decriminalised. And if the Tories could smash the striking miners, who at the time held no small sway on public sympathy, can we in all honestly assume that they couldn't smash a community so widely despised as ours? The memory of the Miners' Strike, coupled with the Race Riots of the early eighties, offers more clues to the motivation of the police as we enter the nineties than any head-count of 'homosexual offences'.

Prior to 1981, the authoritarian populism of Thatcherism provided a fertile ground for the growth of a police *force*, rooted in ideological pessimism and a commitment to uphold the law *at all costs*. Public protest was construed as lawlessness and, in the pivotal case of the striking miners, dissent was criminalised as disorder under the provision of the Public Order Act. Since then, the conspicuous failure of coercive policing to halt rising crime, coupled with flagging public sympathy, has led to a serious change of face at Scotland Yard. In the reconstruction of a model of consensual policing (illustrated by the establishment of police-community consultative groups, the emphasis on Neighbourhood Watch schemes), the police are asking the public to regard them, not as a *force*, but as a *service*. And if the coveted image of a benevolent guarantor of social order is not entirely persuasive nor, any longer, is the notion that the police are simply a monolithic bloc of fascist bootboys.

GALOP (the Gay London Policing Group) have come in for some heavy criticism over their decision to open up dialogue with the Metropolitan police. So too have the dozen or so other community groups who make up the London Lesbian And Gay Policing Initiative - a coalition of representatives who meet with officers at the Yard every three months to thrash out concerns about policing practice in the capital. The most popular charge is that any verbal exchange with the police is, as it were, a cop-out. (It's easier to call someone else a scab than to get off your arse and assist the casualties. When did the Lesbian and Gay Freedom Movement actually *do* anything?)

It may yet transpire that the Met regards the LLGPI as a half-way house, a public relations exercise and no more. Certainly for every move forward (the implementation of pilot schemes to monitor queerbashing attacks) there is another step back (the reference to paedophilia in the revised guidelines for importuning operations). But even a public relations exercise indicates that the police have finally recognised us as *public* beings (in spite of our refusal to comport ourselves *quietly and with dignity*). What the meetings have indicated beyond any reasonable doubt is that the police, far from being the puppets of some omnipotent homophobe in the House of Commons, are actually struggling with an identity crisis on a par with Pinocchio. And what this means (aside from the fact that we should only expect them to indulge in the odd lie or two) is that as we shift towards a United Europe, and personal liberty climbs higher on the political agenda, the good old British bobby is bound to be feeling the pull of a number of interested parties including ours.

Come that day, we'll be glad of those homosexuals who were willing to sacrifice a few political cred-points and bed down with the Boys in Blue.

THE MONTREAL CHARTER

Preamble
HIV disease (infection with HIV with or without symptoms) is a world-

wide epidemic affecting every country. People are infected, sick and struggling to stay alive. Their voices must be heard and their special needs met. This declaration sets forth the responsibilities of all peoples, governments, international bodies, multi-national corporations, and health care providers to ensure the rights of all people living with HIV disease.

Demands

1 All governments and all international and national health organisations must treat HIV disease positively and aggressively as a chronic, manageable condition. Ensuring access and availability of treatment must be part of the social and moral obligations of governments to their citizens.

2 Governments must recognise that HIV disease is not highly infectious. Casual contact presents no threat of infection, and irrational fears of transmission must be fought.

3 An international code of rights must acknowledge and preserve the humanity of people with HIV disease. This code must include:
a) anti-discrimination legislation protecting the jobs, housing and access to services of people with HIV disease;
b) active involvement of the affected communities of people with HIV disease in decision-making that may affect them;
c) guaranteed access to approved and experimental drugs and treatments, and quality medical care;
d) the right to anonymous and absolutely confidential HIV testing. Pre and post counselling must be available;
e) the right to medically appropriate housing;
f) no restriction on the international movement and/or immigration of people with HIV disease;
g) full legal recognition of lesbian and gay relationships;
h) no mandatory testing under any circumstances;
i) no quarantine under any circumstances;
j) protection of the reproductive rights of women with HIV disease, including their right to freely choose the birth and spacing of their children and have the information and means to do so;
k) special attention to the unique problems and needs of injecting drug users, including provision of substance-abuse treatment on demand;

l) special attention to the unique problems and needs of prisoners with HIV disease and guarantees that they will receive the same standard of care and treatment as the general population;

m) the right to communication and all services concerning HIV disease in the language (written, signed or spoken) of his/her choice, through an interpreter if necessary;

n) the provision of reasonable accommodation in services and facilities for disabled people;

o) catastrophic/immunity rights - the guaranteed right of people faced with a life-threatening illness to choose treatments they deem beneficial for themselves.

4 A multi-national, international data bank to make available all medical information related to HIV disease must be created. This includes all data concerning drugs and treatments, especially basic bio-medical research and the initiation of any progress of clinical trials.

5 Placebo trials must be recognised as inherently unethical when they are the only means of access to particular treatments.

6 Criteria for the approval of drugs and treatments should be standardised on an international basis so as to facilitate worldwide access to new drugs and treatments.

7 International education programs outlining comprehensive sex information supportive of all sexual orientations in culturally sensitive ways and describing safer sex and needle use practices and other means of preventing HIV transmission must be made available.

8 The unequal social position of women affecting their access to information about HIV transmission must be recognised and also their rights to programs redressing this inequality, including respect for women's right to control their own bodies.

9 Industrialised nations must establish an international development fund to assist poor and developing countries to meet their health care responsibilities including the provision of condoms, facilities for clean blood supply and adequate supplies of sterile needles.

10 It must be recognised that in most parts of the world, poverty is a critical co-factor in HIV disease. Therefore, conversion of military spending worldwide to medical health and basic social services is necessary.

Editor: Michael Christie. Research and conversations: Chris Woods. Design: Derek Westwood.

I would like to thank: Pascal Brannan, Paul Burston, Dr. Matthew Helbert, Neil McKenna, Bob Mellors, Malcolm Sutherland, Peter Tatchell, and my friend H.B. (who thought of the title), for all their help.

The extract from *Ruling Passions* by Tom Driberg is reproduced by kind permission from Quartet and the Estate.

Alexander Walker's review of *Edward II* in *The Evening Standard*, and subsequent correspondence, is reproduced by permission of Alexander Walker and *The Evening Standard*.

I would also like to thank *Capital Gay* and *The Pink Paper* for permission to reproduce headlines and extracts.

Derek Jarman
January 1992

acknowledgments